Sotheby's International Poetry Competition

D1785482

1982 ANTHOLOGY

Selected by

GWENDOLYN BROOKS · MICHAEL BALDWIN
GEORGE BARKER · BASIL BUNTING
ADRIAN MITCHELL · PETER REDGROVE
STEPHEN SPENDER

Arvon Foundation

First published in Great Britain 1984
by **Arvon Foundation**
Totleigh Barton, Sheepwash, Beaworthy
Devon EX21 5NS

Worldwide Copyright © 1984 by Arvon Foundation Ltd
Worldwide Copyright ©

ISBN 0 9509321 0 8

Typeset and Printed by Penwell Ltd.,
Parkwood, Callington, Cornwall.

Contents

Sotheby's International Poetry Competition 1982

on behalf of the

Arvon Foundation

Sotheby's Prizes

FIRST PRIZE

£5,000

SECOND PRIZE **£4,000**

THIRD PRIZE **£3,000**

FOURTH PRIZE **£2,000**

FIFTH PRIZE **£1,000**

DUNCAN LAWRIE PRIZES
20 PRIZES OF £250 EACH

ARVON FOUNDATION PRIZES
10 PRIZES OF £100 EACH

Judges

GWENDOLYN BROOKS · GEORGE BARKER
BASIL BUNTING · STEPHEN SPENDER
MICHAEL BALDWIN
ADRIAN MITCHELL · PETER REDGROVE

Sponsors

SOTHEBY'S
DUNCAN LAWRIE LIMITED

Introduction

This anthology is a selection from the poems entered for the Sotheby's International Poetry Competition 1982, the second International Poetry Competition organised by the Arvon Foundation.

As with the first Competition anthology, we have removed the names of the authors of each poem to the end of the book, and arranged the poems in alphabetical order of their titles. Readers, if they wish, can act judge. The 89 poems, 35 of which won prizes, were selected from 33,000 poems entered for the 1982 Competition.

The selection, of prize-winners and of runners-up, was made by the Competition judges: Gwendolyn Brooks, Michael Baldwin, George Barker, Basil Bunting, Adrian Mitchell, Peter Redgrove and Stephen Spender.

The Arvon Foundation acknowledges with gratitude the very generous sponsorship and support provided by Sotheby's and by Duncan Lawrie Limited.

A Book of Hard Loving

I.   My hand like a crab along the sea's
backbone, your tide aches.
I ask for water a parchment sun.
My tongue lags
along your thigh.
Greedy I dabble in a last
light before the moon breaks you.

II.   Tomorrow we'll take up
the tournament, the words
I eat you with.
It is always sea-spinning
our hot love that dares
this trawl, the deepest
breach of tongues.

III.   My hollow gut hooks fish
with bright eyes, they spawn
along my side like agents
of a sea as hot and red
as coral, my nightly carnivor.

IV.   Tight as this word I wait
for the wash of dawn the
page flooding

V.   Whisper its not enough
to close up darknesses, your
lip a hungry starfish
mouths our washed beach
The sheet is red you said
whisper the gods will hear

VI.   The seeding undergrowth lets fly
a negative of you, your hands
like glue scaling my thigh
a captured rasp of skins
the bible cracks

VII.   Woods thicken, stars erupt
How to whisper your name it is
a box bursting its lock
And so I ink you in
each flesh-knot rings with
promises of our unravelling

VIII.   High over voices the flesh
leans on
I match your face to page
and skins howl.
It is a parapet of moons
a star-curved hill
If I were hare I'd conjure you
to race this night with me.
If I were berry I'd crack
beneath you heel.
But I've enough sweet juices
and my foot is tough for
hawking, for this land's
blistering.

IX.   If I were many times myself
I'd clothe your neck and ring
you with a smile that is
my widest opening.
Split rock beneath the axe
your mouth my knave my oh so
brave and moonstruck forester
is traps

A Citizen in a Monastery

Two miles above the sea in a silent monastery
Unpaced by monk or visitor, I sit at a long concrete refectory table
And look out on tranquillity. Above me, spreading over
                                the inhabitation,
Is a giant plane tree, big enough to cool a village square.
The blue sea stretches away and the green hills sweep upwards,

8

The sun beats down and the birds sing in the incense-scented
                                        pine trees.
The cells of the monks are still and the shadowed courtyard
Dappled with a cool warmth, the warmth of June.
Around me roar the wars, both upwards and downwards,
And on all sides, the bloody logic irrefutable,
The law of cause and effect furious and bloody,
There is no end, human on human, like trains shooting
                                        into tunnels
They pursue inevitable doom. O holy God,
To you, who made the atom, inlaid the principles of
                                        ladders and watermelons,
Who comprehends insanity, swims in the blood of the unborn,
Who touches conception, increases without constriction,
Who has no trouble with mathematics, nor can misunderstand
                                        astrophysics,
Who implicitly rejected emptiness yet made it your very own
                                        doorstep;
To you, who focus sharply on everything, like the
                                        glassed eye of a jeweller,
Unbamboozled by perspective, unconcerned about motion
Nor the terrible traffic in explosions dotting the infinite;
To you, like the finger of a peasant woman pushing a thimble
Driving the inscrutable steel that patches up division,
Who loves the infant instinct to prayer and the awkwardness
                                        of adults
Congregating in their crash-helmets of self-consciousness;
To you, the glory of the world, at last I come
To ravish my own self with the paradox you inhabit
And I must transcribe, foreordained by Permission.
You are my mighty dictator and I am here unworthily
Scratching dictation, a blue pen on a white page,
Unhurried to begin, nor impatient to continue,
                                        your ever loving secretary,
Summoned from drunkeness and the inscooping orbits of
                                        pretty women,
Dazzled by opportunity, crushed by the gravity of it all,
But functioning, apprehensive, ready.

   I sing the Unsplit God, the father adamantine,
The furious bastard, the lethal witch, the administrator,
The stinking origin, the foul-mouthed, yellow-belly poisoning.
I sing the trap-door cunning, the round-the-corner back-up;

The double-cross, the deceit; the lazer whip, and the horses
Molten gold them all, flowing in the rivers of precession.
I praise how the marble of mountains and the cotton wool
           of doctors
Coexist in the world of the kneecap of the Almighty.
I praise the vigil, the career, and the compassion
Peopled in conference in the lip of the Aforesaid.
I praise the jail, the injustice, and the juror
Battling it out in the elbow the Unsplit God is scratching.
I praise the rain, the lightning flash, and the thunder
An incident in his fingernail he taps for amusement.
  See here the story of first beginnings,
A concrete bench and a morning-glory flower
Co-exact, even as the mournful purple of bougainvillea
Heaves into radiance. See here now
The monastery is to the pill-box what tranquillity is to
         the machine-gun.
Both have their purpose, you say. But I say, Not so.
The pill-box and the machine-gun have their purpose,
But the monastery and the tranquillity are at the end of purpose.
For this is the edge of the world, the plane tree fluttering.
For this is the vigil of mankind, the senior hiding-place,
The refuge of the scholar, the saint, and the scoundrel.

  A copper bell hangs in the branches of a tree.
An empty chair in the courtyard faces the sea where waves
Like sub-atomic particles in a cloud-separation chamber
Sink to oblivion, and the edge of the sea is tinted aquamarine.
The monastery is deserted (brandy bottles strewn below
         the foundations)
Except for the closed doors of five monks at prayer.
      On a neighbouring hill
The radar of the army turns swiftly in the heat.
Soldiers dine. A fishing vessel hugs the coastline. I hear
The cry of the tortured, those instantly maimed, and the dead,
The lacerated, the burned, the dying, and the unloved.
The song of the freed, the miraculous recoverer, the
        enchanted parent,
The lucky, the friends in wild bars, the loving and the trustful
Help soothe imagination, but What is going on ? is the
       only real question.

  The wind shakes early fruit from a tree. The sun casts
       no shadow.

A private yacht assaults the entire blue of the sea.
Courting birds flash between treetops. Even the rubbish sparkles
And a wild goat with gold eyes and a shaggy coat
Enters the dappled courtyard. The trunk of the tree, hollow,
And big enough to house a children's party,
Grows out of the ground with the massive conviction of
                                      an elephant's foot.
The boney elbows of the giant boughs uphold a starry
                                        dome of leaves
Intertinted with the palest of blues sparkling at the zenith.
A hemisphere of water in a glass shivers on the concrete table top
And loose crumbs of bread blow hither and thither in the
                                     uncertain wind.

     Here in a cell where the air is dark and quiet
Light flows through with the glowing information of the sun.
The uneven whitewashed walls stand two feet thick.
The cell is furnished by silence.
Outside, the local insect population
Seethes on its urgent mission, and the hooves of goats
Can be heard running along a wall. Truth is how
One man's life finds peace in such a place
Looking out on the sea beneath the shadow of the fruit trees
Footed and shouldered by hills, visited by birds,
Drinking from a well of clear water in the uncut rock,
Stable in body and mind, praying with others
Morning, noon, and evening beneath the all-inspiring plane tree.
Nothing can collapse in the atmosphere of prayer.
Murder cannot move the peace which comes with love.

Adam Naming the Creatures

My tongue, the new spade to dig through
the acres of namelessness,
Genesis' lush and dreaming mud.
In exhalation, there will be names.
In logos, dominion and order.
Word-skins to fit the creatures
in the cacophony of spinning dark:

11

You will be *Snail*, *I am who I carry*,
I am who I shield, with tentacles quivering
in sleep on the Hiddekel's* oozing banks.
And you, the sister called *Turtle*,
who wears a leathery sadness,
whose labour rocks out a glisten of eggs,
small moons for these first nights.

And *Fox*, his fur burnished by hot wind,
he lies down, flashing blue-white tendons,
his teeth a snare for the grape and the meat.
He broods over a rookery
of feather-sticks, who are *Birds*,
the grass of prehistory in their claws.

Birds, with wings that flash through the sky,
do you weave air out of yourselves,
or does the air extrude you
to this wildest, speckled firmament?
Free, *free*, *free*, you clatter:
Who looks at you shall be moved with flight.

And *Bear*, ursus, the brown-gummed dreamer
eating up his own fat
in the stinking chamber of winter sleep;
he who consumes himself, yet lives,
who wakes up with hunger smeared
on his dripping jaws.

And I, frail bone shaking in this new world,
I live by my syllables and vowels
that, rising, richochet through
the glare of palmettos.
With the fat and protein of these words,
I increase myself, attaching names
like second carapaces, shells and fins.
The cosmos thrums, beating with the noise
of flying and crouching,
their hissing and climbing.

river named in Genesis

12

You will be *Bats*, flutter-mice,
with greasy sails on finger bones,
whose upside down sleep
invades ours like an incubus,
innocents with defiled and defiling faces.
Fly quietly past *Giraffe*
of the long blue tongue,
past *Walrus*, who walks on her own tusks.

And *Whale*, out there on the seething waters,
with mound shaped like desire,
who bleeds grey to color the ocean,
whose bright saliva is the waves' crest:
contralto, warbler in the longest miles
of opera, muted under fathoms.

And how shall I describe the carrion?
Or the creature of coiled knowledge
that crept into me
on its diamond-studded back?
Through time, I shall bruise its head,
and it shall bruise my heel.

And you I call *Beaver, I am teeth that grow forever,*
who must always gnaw to trim them down —
or mouths blocked, die in streams, unable to eat.
Pity such a killing growth
that would starve by its own vigor.

And poised near the streams are *Deer*,
evanescents, with eyes
the very cups of trembling,
whose tails glow like new clouds,
as they graze on ferns rooting deep
in the shock of this rising sun.

And you, tainted black pig of the world,
understand the we —
the tribe of sky-searching,
upward-walking shafts of flesh —
we will never love you.
You must drag across the world,
this sty of pain,

by your own haunches, your own dumb bulk,
past pitch and tar and slime,
while we lurch above you,
spectators of the animal chaos,
and all that is animal within —
while we watch you rut and bask and lie
in the green carbon forest,
denying that the shine of grime
in your scarred eyes
is the grimy light in ours:
Oh son, misbegotten, oh daughter, ours.

A Halifax Cider Jar

Digging

Isaac;
The last potter in Halifax,
Old man boot-thumping his spade through tussocks,
Stacking turves, scraping topsoil,
Exposing the endless coal-seam measure of clay.

Back bent, shirt sweated to thin vertebrae,
He grunt-heaves shovelsful to the rusting
Model-T truck, the ochre element lifting
To his slow deliberation, untiring sinew.

At pit-bottom a pool swallows
Spinning sky in reflection,
Gobbles tumbling crumbs from his labour;
He pauses only to hawk and spit,
Staring at the moor-edge before him
Where grass and harebells bend
Under kiln-draughting wind.

Behind him, in his blood's dizziness,
The pottery chimney sways:

His heart hovers, beating
Like lark-choirs above.

Clay drags at feet and shovel until
His very skull is dull with suction,
Until spade and final spadeful
Are tossed in the truck,
And he drags free his barkled boots,
Clambers up into the cab,
Yanks and kicks the engine
From its black sulleness,
Till it runs, jolting and roaring
And protesting, up Soil Hill.

Blunging

The blunger is waiting, octagonal, water-heavy;
Isaac, balanced on his truckload of clay, leans
To shift the lever that engages flat-belts,
Begins its iron gut-churnings, then shovels
In the load with its sheepshit and frogspawn,
The huge-bellied, cast-iron maw
Barely swallowing.

Above him heavy gear-teeth sleepwalk,
Knitting in their black grease,
Driving the paddle in the iron tub
With the force of shifting bedrock.

In the whirlpool-swallow
Clay chunks appear and disappear,
Stones clank on the dull sides,
Tines turn unstoppably:
Nightmare of centrifuge,
Maelstrom of Creation, melting
And re-forming always in
Its own turbulent image.

The potter has his pipe going, stands
On the banking in the breeze-chill
Of the swept moors, watching until satisfied.

He jumps down and heaves the stop-cock open:
Slurry bursts through the sieve
As through a wrecked dyke,
Leaving heather roots
And pebbles that glaciers buried.

The flood surges in its plank channel,
Enters the long drying beds
Where its settles slowly,
Stands thickening,
The hot kiln flues beneath drawing
Off its moisture like breath.

Pugging

The clay has cracked across —
Lake-beds in drought,
Sacrificial badlands.

Isaac kneels in his boiler-suit
And pokes in a finger,
Feeling clay as if it were tobacco
Or fine cloth,
Making sure it will come down
To his measure.

He prises dead-weight chunks
From the hot bats —
Sticky, warm clay-stench —
Slaps them in the barrow
And trundles through the pottery
His grandfather framed, building
Under wind's vigilance from
Earth's coals and clays.

At the pug-mill, with a potshard,
Issac cleans off the chunks,
Scraping dust, stuck leaves, blown grit,
Forcing lumps down the iron mouth
Onto intestinal blades:
Their heedless kniving draws
To quick digestion, hours

At the wedging table in minutes
Churned out by hundredweights
As the mill shits clay;
Isaac measures the slow bar
With expert eye, wiring
Off perfect weights, which
Stacked to sour slow months,
He re-pugs and sours again,
Until his satisfaction
Fingers it for the wheel.

Throwing

This is the moment that machines
Have toiled to:
Isaac lifts the two-stone ball of clay
And smacks it on the wheelhead,
His foot prods forward,
Drive-cones engage
And the wheel turns.

His hands, dipped at the tray
As if by afterthought,
Grip the cold clay and press
With subtle conviction, centring the mass.
As he feels it give to centrifuge,
His hand, beginning the mystery,
Has already shaped a hole
That presently, elbow deep,
Opening out,
Swallows his entire arm.

He knuckles up the belly,
Lifting weight high for balance,
Coaxing walls just thick enough,
Smoothing with an iron rib,
Then bringing in wide shoulders,
Enclosing darkness, his desire
Concentrating
Clay to the neck:

A sudden quickening,
Fingers slipping the moist hole
That harvesters' dreg-galled lips
Will rest at, until,
Withdrawing delicately,
The wheel slowing,
Stillness,
It is done.

Fettling

Cut from the wheelhead with a wire,
Lifted with a cow's rib,
The jar stands drying, fussed
From pot-board to pot-board,
Checked for cracks and warps,
Until Isaac lifts it, green hard —
Still plastic to finger prints —
And rests it in his crooked arm,
His thumb smoothing off ragged clay
Where the wire dragged.

Deftly he cuts tap-hole
And spiggot-hole;
His hand-heel dimps
The base concave,
Its dull note already sounding.

Resting the jar down,
He takes two turds of clay,
Which wetted, he fashions,
Pulling and pressing
And coaxing
Into handles
On either side;

Ears harkening
At liquid darkness.

Glazing

The jar has dried —
Ochre pollen-dust;
Astride his pancheons of glaze
Isaac ladles in a jugfull.

He grips handles,
Sways from the waist
In his leather apron,
Spinning the jar on his wrists,
Red-lead washing each hidden belly-rib
It will convert.

But for the outside
Isaac keeps a richer glaze:
He ups the jar and dips it
Shoulder deep, to the apex-curve
In galena, making a caul
That will burn-sheen his ware
With forgotten depth.

Once more it is stood to dry,
Sleepy, grey-white,
The whole jar dozing
To dullness;

A legend
Awaiting the flame
Of its coming.

Firing

Isaac has built up the fire-boxes,
Stacked the kiln altar-pyre
With dried ware; now he bricks up
The wicket, daubing ash and wet clay
To make a seal.

Six fire-mouths:
At each he touches match to paper,
Feels wind whipping flame from his fingers,

19

Down-draughting through flues to the high stack
That teeters on the moor-rim.

For the last time he sweats in the hovel,
Stoking purgatorial heat through long
Miracle-making hours, searing his pots
With alchemy, a thousand degrees of heat
Burning out their clay-dross
To redemption.

After tons of coal-heaving Isaac
Draws out the peep-hole brick, sets
His eye to sheer incandescence:
Sees melted signal cones,
The yellow-blind glare,
And so seals up the fires
And goes home to sleep,
Kiln-heat sinking day by day.

It is dawn when he breaks down the wall,
Riving at brickwork and baked clay until
Light strikes upon the constellation
Of stacked pots, each a supernova,
A star-fire prodigy,
Earthenware flaming deep red,
Honey-brown glaze gleaming
Like combs in a broken hive.

Isaac reaches for the cider jar —
Still hot — rests it for inspection
In the warming crook of his arm,
Fingering the dappled glaze
Where his smile deepens.

He sets it down, strikes
Its sweet note against pottery flagstones,
Then turns to emptying kiln's harvest,
Knowing no more of it under the years' attrition
Than of himself:

Isaac,
Bones under winds' keening,

The drenched burial place
Over-cried by curlews.

Soil Hill
An atrocity of moorland,
Roof sagging, kiln crumbling,
Carcase that gales fast on.

This cider jar
Still brimming with darkness
From his touch.

All over the world

women are knitting
in Ireland they are knitting thick
creamy cables each with their special stitch
so when their man is dragged out of the sea
with his face bloated purple
they will know him

in New York they are knitting on subways
with bright orange yarn stitch after
stitch and folding up their needles
tucking them into the plastic bag inside
a flowered plastic tote
in time to the train wheels as
the subway stops and they get off

in England they are knitting in airports
not only the English the Indians
the Pakistani the Americans they are
all sitting in Heathrow Airport knitting
long indecipherable scarves for persons
unkown

in Italy they are knitting black sweaters
for the saints with the methodical care
they perform upon their rosaries

women in Wales are knitting the dawn into
peat bog afghans girls in Ghana are
knitting tribal chieftans into unimagined
legends women in Chile are knitting
blood into the stockpile of tourniquets
waiting for the next round young women

in Istanbul are knitting far into the future
which is a replica of the past and it keeps
shrinking the closer they move into tomorrow

women in Iran are knitting insignias of the
oil companies to be sewn into the
covers for the coffins women in Ethopia
are knitting green and white and red ribbons
to be worn around the hearts of those who
will not recognize the outcome

women in Russia are knitting peaceful parables
that will win the Nobel Prize
with long slavonic colors of melancholy
and hearty despair

women in Kansas are knitting according to the
latest catalogue in yellow and white
they are knitıng strands of wheat into their
needles and they will
fill their kitchens with the abundance
that smiles because Kansas has not been bloody
since the time of the fierce old man John Brown

women in Amsterdam are knitting blue and white
porcelain doilies that are brittle and break
quickly unless purchased by tourists
their daughters are knitting with the
precision of an etching deep brown
quilts to cover themselves and their
lovers against the piercing sky

women in Paris are knitting bright Picasso
sweaters that they will never wear because
even now they do not know what makes them
choose those colors

women in the swamps and rivers of Indochina
are knitting the reeds and nettles into the
steel of machine gun bullets that will
explode with warmth into the bodies of
the men that are cold with the ignorance
of trespassing and long for comfort

girls in vacant towns
inbetween cities inbetween rivers on
maps are knitting their hopes in
small stitches echoing into each other
like muffled mirrors the needles
click smoothly in that language all
of the same word over and over
that no one can read the
same word over and over

Aurelius

ONE

Gold Aurelius, the captain of a pirate ship,
With a hold full of captive girls,
Tethered with threads of gold,
Sitting naked among the pineapples and the melons.
Brought from the Indies, all heading safe
For home . . .
         . . . and Green Aurelius, strolling round
The Happy Valley New Estate,
Watches young couples come to view
His half-built houses. He hears a fiancée plan
A patio, a kitchen suite; the clay
Will sprout gardens, the dangling electric wires
Refrigerators and washing machines. Gold
Will turn in his pocket to green. Then he hurries back,
Chauffer-driven to his luncheon-date,
To meet important backers at the King's.
Talking on, through coffee and liqueurs,
About his plans, unfinished deals,
Expansion schemes, his company's ships . . .
         . . . which Gold Aurelius homeward steers.

TWO

Red Aurelius, rising at the dawn
And striding across the windswept land,
Hunting with gold-eyed hounds
Until the night comes down;
And lies with arrows by the river-bank
For the lovely, gliding swan . . .
    . . . and Black Aurelius,
All week amid the noise of pistons,
The talk of engineers and old blue jokes,
Told between the beers and teas and cigarettes.
Now at last, his overalls off, climbing
With the other cars the hill and looking back
At all the chimneys left behind;
The fumes of factories drifting flat
Across the sky, but up above,
A fine Arabian sickle moon, a frieze of stars
This cloudless night. His headlamps shine,
Among the shadows of the fields . . .
    . . . on Red Aurelius and his hounds.

THREE

Brown Aurelius, plant-juice painted,
Tells the stories of his race;
Sees devils in the moonlit space
And truant children in the stars.
Sees coming down the river troops
And overhead the bomber-planes . . .
    . . . and White Aurelius
Enters by the marble stair,
The cool corridor and the panelled door;
Controls five ringing telephones,
Confers with Secretaries of State
About his ministry's special cares,
(Calls through at lunch-time to inquire
The price of South American rubber shares)
Signs memoranda designed to cause
Reform of boundaries in Rutlandshire,
And works on late. Until at nine,

He drives away from Whitehall's
Floodlit, ivory flanks . . .
      . . . and Brown Aurelius finds the jungle
                  full of tanks.

FOUR

Blue Aurelius, flinging back
His rainbow hair from that
Pale, creamy maiden's face of his,
Earns another thousand screams,
A thousand pounds, yet sings
Of peace and love and poverty . . .
      . . . and Grey Aurelius
Went to the abbot with his plans
To build a great church in the Fens,
Where God would be worshipped all the years.
Stone from Purbeck, stone from Cork,
A thousand masons worked for him.
In later years the monk grew grim
And turned May dancers into stone
For singing on a Holy day — the legend says —
And hated troubadours. Yet still a mason
Carved two laughing imps, pick-a-back,
Above his tomb, facing where the meadows lie,
Spread with tents this festival . . .
      . . .where Blue Aurelius comes to sing,
                  for Charity.

FIVE

Violet Aurelia parades before the aging King,
Lets slip her veils one by one,
Until, the morsels of her body bare,
She stands, her flesh as soft
As if just licked to shape
By some huge, tender mother-bear . . .
      . . . and Pink Aurelia
Learnt to fight when she was young,
When bullies crowded her against
The plain green railings of the school. A man
Made love to her at sweet sixteen

And left her with a howling son. And now,
At thirty-five, she takes her pleasure where she can,
Her lovers sometimes call her hard,
But breaks as easily as a shell
To crying when she's on her own.
She writes, crusades in print each Sunday morning,
Against Injustice, Poverty, Mis-Education
Of the Young; across the page, a photo shows . . .
      . . . Miss V. Aurelia's latest pose.

SIX

Gold Aurelius forces naked girls ashore
In shivering lines along the dock
Against a background of tall cranes;
Pays off his crew who grumbling go
Towards the beds of prostitutes, then drives away
And is saluted at the gates . . .
      . . . Aurelius without a name
Sleeps in the darkened quiet ward,
Fed and washed and given sedatives,
And kept indoors. "I went out long ago
But all the colours dazzled me,
Of cars and shops and summer clothes,
And young girls' bodies almost bare,
The affluence of Power there.
So now I stay inside and dream
Of childhood holidays by the sea, of cottage-windows
Bright with sun. I let the doctors pamper me
And get up sometimes in the afternoons,
But will not read the newspapers . . ."
      . . . and Green Aurelius stands for Parliament.

Bible Story

When Lot and the children were past, she shook herself
and salt sprang off like water. The wide plain shone
in the setting sun, and a breeze blew up. Birds sang.
She stepped forth naked, not shy; her nakedness
making her red mouth smile. She was all over
consistency of plum. These legs, these thighs,
this belly, these breasts, these shoulders belonged to her.
Birdsong, and the sun down; stars, and no angel's moon.
She flicked her long black glossy salt-washed hair
across her shoulders, breasts; and felt a fire
(not a destroying fire, nor purifying)
leaping between her legs. In the dry distance
along the road to Zoar, poor earnest Lot
rested, not looking back. Brisk, with new grace,
and tremulous with tender expectation,
she moved back down the road to merry Sodom
now twinkling in the dark.
The wrath of upright angels, the disapproval
of peckish angels, cannot unmake a city,
no matter what you think you may have heard;
dry men in small dull places write as they please.
She'd see again
her fine big house, her friends and frolic neighbors,
the river of exotic travellers,
the cries and colors of the marketplace,
the gardens and granaries. She would invite,
smiling, the merry men, farmers and merchants,
poets and artisans, alive in Sodom.
To be alive, and like a ripened plum
in Sodom! Lightly, laughing, she came home.

California Photograph

A chair is placed on the edge of the continent for my
        great grandfather.
And there he sits, the captain, his paternity, his
        vigorous festivals of faith,
His skills in personal compromise thrown out beneath
        his gaze;
While on his left a table with a checkered cloth holds
        black grapes,
And on the right his rifle, gripped with easy hand,
        persisting in his skull,
Beneath the broad-rimmed hat, some cooling celebrations.

How spirited and commanding is his accommodation of
        a multiplicity of views.
How strong his chord of final point of melody within
        this scene
Bold tanner of wild hides and lover of dark women
        closes here
A funny little destiny, a moral fugue, an harmonic
        calculation
That men are not among the grander paraphernalia of
        the earth.
And we, having slipped beyond his recollection, are
        addressed and properly, as strangers
Now that he has seen and heard the sea.

Can't Make It

To tell you the truth, I don't think I can make it.
I stare into all-night delis, into bars and fast food joints
As if they're scenes from a movie, pictures of Mars,
And I feel flattened, buried in a used car graveyard,
Talking to myself with a tongue of scrap metal.

I dream that busloads of people are screaming with grief,
And I long for the warmth of an electric blanket.
I want to forget burst pipes, shopping malls, bus stations,
And the bleakness of army camps on Sunday afternoon.

I can't stand all these crammed bookshelves.
I'm avoiding my felt tip pen, typewriter, sweater vest,
My T-shirt, wallet, wrinkles, contact lenses.

It would be different if I were a good dancer,
Or had an athlete's body, or the face of a movie star;
I'd have liked girls to fall on me if I offered a smile;
It's no good dying of love while posterity
Watches pro football or plays electronic games.

The past keeps coming after me like a perpetual motion machine
Cranking out tears and reprimands, falling on its knees,
Sobbing over my dead lives like an Italian mother.
It forces me out at night into wet streets.
I stare at fire escapes, water tanks, microwave towers,
At blackened bricks that long to get down from the walls,
To stretch out and sleep in the street like old winos.

I see unhappiness in stores that have failed,
Lonely interiors stripped of racks and merchandise;
I remember lamps that no longer light, stored in closets,
And exhausted house plants, dropping leaves like large tears.

I pick myself up like a wounded gangster:
"Mother of Mercy, is this the end of Rico?"
Tougher than I thought, I smile, I flirt,
Joking with pretty girls who have blank eyes,
Who have already seen darkness falling,
Who have seen enough, who want to look no more.

Casual Labour

1 . A half-acre breeze-block shell,
     hygienically chill. Five men in white.
     The tall bandsaw beside us
     is flaking blue, cast iron.
     Someone backs the trailer:
     we see an elongating cube
     within the walls' grey planes.
     The veiled carcases spill.
     Strip their frozen muslin.
     Saw them into shopping.

2 . Alloy tubes and metal-banded boards
     to be unshackled, sorted, stored.
     Arm over arm, the lengths slide.
     Bolts are freed and tested, slung in bins.
     A building has come clear
     of our attentions, finished verticals
     independent of this crazy puzzle.
     The platforms and the drops,
     the high rooms without walls,
     all come away, the sheeting falls,
     and us jaunty chimps
     swing down and piss off home,
     dragging our knuckles.

3 . Arrangement of pallets.
     With a grid of orders
     and a hydraulic hand truck,
     alter the arrangement.

4 . Peel blue polythene from sheets of steel,
     reveal dull mirrors.
     Tubes of light overhead
     shudder and warp as I strip their reflections.
     These thin plates are sharp:
     my fingerprints are scored.
     The radio won't work:
     this building is charged to the ceiling
     with a static of fine metal.
     I am perfecting the deft system

of myself as the process
by which the polythene is peeled . . .
and someone wheels away another stack.

5 .   The depot's quiet.
Out at the waste fire
near the perimeter
all the imperatives loosen.
I've stashed the heavy tools
and shed my boiler suit.
I crouch in jeans, play primitive,
watching for the chargehand through the flames,
and stepping clear, I jump the fire
again, again, trying out this brighter skin
in the risk of wild light.
Then I choose the safety clothes,
kick soil on the fire, return
to the terminal buildings.

Chicken Feathers

1

What a picture!
She has tucked her wild-looking chicken
under her arm and stares out
over what seems to be a mountain pass
on a windy day.
She is wearing a blue linen dress
the colour of summer.
She reminds me of Brunhilde—
alone,bronzed,unfamiliar.
She doesn't look like anybody's mother.

2

She used to love dancing.
She went to the Chelsea Ball
dressed as a leopard;

there she met my father,
who looked so dashing
in the Harlequin suit
his tailor made for him
from raw silk.
He had tiny shoes
like Cinderella's.
I have seen them.

3

She comes to collect me from school,
on time, silent,
and I hand her my coat and satchel—
avoiding,even then,her lovely eyes,
that look down on my world
like distant stars.
I play with the girl next door,
and don't come home till bed-time.

4

From the lighted window
I watch my mother
picking leeks in the twilight.

I will have soup
for my supper,
sprinkled with parsley.

She passes me my creamy bowl.
My hands are warm,
and smell of soap.

My mother's hands are cold as roots.
She shuts up the chickens
by moonlight.

5

How can they think I am asleep
when he bends down and kisses
the nape of her neck,
and goes away to his own room,
while she sits in front of her mirror
and brushes and brushes
her waist-long silver hair?

6

The hens are all gone.
How happy she used to be
setting out in her long tweed coat
across the orchard
with her bucket.
Chuck,chuck,chuck,she called
and they'ld all come running.

7

She walks behind the hedges
of the large garden,stooping
from time to time
to pick narcissi
for her mother's grave,
now that it is Easter.
We don't want to go.
We're too young to remember
our grand-mother—
and besides it will be cold
in the grave yard
where the wind blows
straight in off the downs.

8

He went to his room with an orange
in his hand,and died there
sometime during the afternoon.
My mother spent the day in the kitchen.
When I came in from the garden
I was sent upstairs
to call him down to tea:
He was sitting by the window
with his back to me.
On the table beside him
were four boats made of orange peel,
with the pith piled neatly inside them.

My mother couldn't stand up.
She kept on saying she was sorry,
but she couldn't stand up.
'It must be the shock'she said.
It wasn't grief.
'Come and sit down'she said,
'and have your tea.'

9

Tonight I kissed my mother,
for the first time that I can remember;
though I must have kissed her before,
as all daughters kiss their mothers.

She was passing in front of me
to kiss the children,and I leant down
and touched her cheeks with my lips.
It was easy—like the lighting of a candle.

10

My sister always says
that on the morning our father died
he was working on a drawing of a liner
disappearing over a white horizon.
She says it is a symbol.
She's got the picture by her bed.
I would rather think of dying
as a coming into harbour,
a sort of final mooring.

11

You put in at a little jetty.
There is some-one there to welcome you—
not sinister—but rather surprising—
some-one you know. In front of you rise
banks of fern and shining celandines.
You can smell the woods.
They are full of life,
but very still.

12

My mother and I,in our way,
understand one another.
When I kneel by her grave,
in need of a little consolation,
I will picture her standing
on a hillside in bright sunlight,
lifting her hand to wave to me;
or is she brushing away the feathers
that drift like dreams into her hair
and tickle her cheek,till she smiles.

Cockerel

His shout bangs
Rivets through a tin shed roof.
One foot holds the world in handcuffs.

Above his shanty town he
Pins on medals; President
Pole-Star.

A constellation of dull wives
Divides to let him through.
Someone must kiss this raised foot.

Above him the sun is
Balancing her weights.
His hatred for its providence grows.
Satanic is how that makes him feel.
His neck blooms red with anger.

To get the better of words
He is learning to read.
Even in bed he can't get his uniform off.

Each morning this
Silent challenge of the sun.
Each morning
A warm hand on his shoulder. If
Only he could master an alphabet
He might topple the tyrant
Clear out of the sky.

David of the Mines

BOOTS

Boots on the hob for the morning,
Dad's and mine, reflecting
The dying light of
Fire.
The fire that burns my father's
Daily toil.

Black boots for the morning.
School is for sissies and scholars.
Down where the devil chips at the
Mine,
The sun turns and flees from
The dust.

"Mam, I can't sleep for the morning.
Tell me again, of the
Shining new copper-
Penny,
I shall earn scratching at
The face".

"Son, I often long for the morning.
Dad's cough lasts till the
Dawn, coal dust takes our
Men,
And turns them black inside
And out".

Boots on the hob for the morning,
Bread for his tea,
He'll sip water by lamp
Light,
Six and skinny, earn a penny
For me.

THE MORNING

Still dark, I hear the pit wheels whirrling,
Mam is up, the house is stirring.
Dad is slow and never a smile,
He trims his wick for a long long while.
"Mam tie my lace,
See my clean white face,
Kiss me like you do Dad
I'm a miner today and glad".

Squares of light line the miners row,
A doorstep kiss before they go,
Bang shut the door
Both turn to their daily chore.
Men flock from their feather beds,
Like sheep with stars on their heads.
Studded boots strike blue sparks,
An abandoned Jack Russel barks.

Down the deadly shaft, look up if you dare,
The last stars are squashed into a square.
Other boys clad in rags without boots,
Saplings torn out by their roots.
Nightmares feast between ear and eye,
Demons drip from on high.
Yet coal carts roll on out of sight,
Filled with the labour of childrens fright.

BEAUTIFUL BLACK FACE

I strike you beautiful black-face,
Lying on my back.
The fragments fly in my eyes
Blind as a mole
Faced with the sun.

For what seems forever black-face,
I have eaten at you today,
Filled cart after cart,
I, hewer of the coal,
Your elevator to the light.

Water runs down my arm black-face,
Do tears from your liquid eyes,
Wash the graze on my face?
But hear I well the bell,
Home time at last.

Good night my mutilated black-face,
And your propped up mouth.
A shaft of shivering shift boys,
All praying for their supper,
Potatoes please, for dad, mam and me.

SUNDAY AND MARION

Marion lives four doors away,
And goes to school every day,
But on Sundays if it doesn't rain,
We play around in Cobblers Lane.

Sit on the steps and pick at bricks,
Watch the lads and learn new tricks.
Snippets of leather from the cobbler's door,
Or a handful of crumbs from the baker's floor.

So passes Sunday my upright day,
When I can stretch run and play.
I learn to scratch my name on slates,
Climb on walls and swing on gates.

Marion's mam always seems to sew,
The seamstress of the miners' row.
Patch upon patch on a collier's seat,
In return for potatoes, coal and meat.

So we match and make a reckless pair,
I six, she seven and never a care.
Her mam sits spinning wool from a fleece,
Her hands are soft from the old ewes grease.

Next Sunday I shall count to ten,
To spell what, where and when,
She'll show me a book with the A B C
And D for David, that's my name you see.

DAD'S SORTIE

Dad's gone to the mountain tonight,
With his sack and mining light.
I watch from my frosted window
As he climbs and climbs through the snow.

Mam is nervous and stokes the fire,
Prodding it like a funeral pyre,
Hunger pangs rivet other eyes,
They longingly await mutton pies.

Dad's light reappears at our back gate,
Puffing white breath at a poacher's-rate.
Frozen eyebrows like a diamond strip,
His hunch back shows a fruitful trip.

In the coal house the sheep is skinned,
We all know dad has sinned.
Many a fleece is scraped and cured,
Mam's apron is bulging with her hoard.

The women are gathering in a pack,
Like shadows merging into a stack,
Basins, baskets and white enamel bowls
Carry morsels to nourish bodies and souls.

SOMEONE

Someone put the day light out,
Pushed the sun beneath the earth,
Deeper than I ever dug.
Though they say I'll find the light.

Someone put the seasons out,
Spring and summer burst and gone,
Above my moonless night hole,
Where they say the daytime reigns.

Someone put my choldhood out,
Mam still scrubs me in the tub,
Folds me warm before the fire,
She says it draws coal from my pores.

39

Yet, someone put my childhood out,
Like a half told fairy tale,
Exhaustion froze the very myths,
I say I hung my day and night on.

IN BETWEEN

Half a man
Half a boy
Half wrong and
Half right.
Half in boots
Half in bread,
But whole in hours and hardship.

Half in strength
Half in weight
Half alert and
Half asleep.
Half afraid
Half a mind
To mooch today if I could.

ALL WENT SMOOTHLY

All went smoothly,
So to the summer of just Sundays.
    Down the mine,
    Out of the mine,
Time was the coal in the basket.

All went smoothly,
Until a roar from a tunnel of darkness,
    Burst around me,
    Coal bombarded me,
Life lay mangled all around.

All went smoothly,
Trapped behind a rough coal wall,
    Time flopped around,
    Silence smelt around,
Black-face had me in its jaw.

All went smoothly,
The rescue came in handpicked hours,
    Through the dust,
    Till like the dust,
I settled in a miner's arms.

All went smoothly,
Tommy died, in my hand hewn tunnel,
    Beneath the baskets,
    My day's baskets -
Rolled him out of sight,

A DAY IN BED

Today my mam let the sun
Reach the doorstep before her.
The alarm of the passing miners,
Drew me to my window.

Today my mam let me sleep,
Dad had gone hours ago.
I thought of my friend Tommy,
He had earned my rest.

Today my mam dressed in black
And left at ten o'clock.
The oblong coffins elbowed past
Tommy never looked that neat.

Today my mam bathed me well
And told me of her plan,
To send me to Llangynidr,
To stay with my Aunt Nancy.

A POLICEMAN CALLED HE

A policeman is coming up our steps,
Dressed as smart as hell,
Stiff as a frozen boot lace,
And sharp knocks he.

The floorboards of my bedroom gape,
And through them I hear,

Mam and dad and he
In solemn frightening tones.

"I knew it would come to this",
Said my dad.
"But I fed a few poor mouths,
Only too few it seems".

"I've known you for many years",
Said he,
"But I have my orders to carry out,
You have to come with me".

       "Now" said dad,
       "Now" said he,
       "Now" cried mam
       And echoed me.

A policeman is going down our steps,
Dad with his coat on his arm,
Trailing lost like a puppy,
Left our mam stiff, like he.

THE HANGING CHANT

"Your dad's going to swing for the sheep",
By his neck I hear them say,
Up by the road to Llangynidr,
Where the drovers pass along.

"Your dad's going to swing for the sheep",
Mam sits silent and dreams,
Absently darning the woollen socks,
That he will never wear.

"Your dad's going to swing for the sheep",
It's forecast by the Row.
Door to door, verbal slush
Is gobbled up and passed along.

"Your dad's going to swing for the sheep",
Won't do his cough much good.
Mam never leaves the house,
Since he left that night.

"Your dad's going to swing for the sheep",
I shop, cook and clean for mam,
I feel like a mother myself,
And she too young to talk.

PACK IT

Oh pack it mam,
You can't pack the bed
Or the old green rug,
Or the willow pattern bowl and jug.

Oh pack it mam,
The rosey paper on my walls
The window and its sill,
The view that now must stand still.

Oh pack it mam,
My eight years here,
Our kneeling height's the same,
Oh, could I only pack your shame.

Oh pack it mam,
Must I really go away?
I whisper this in my head,
I know, it must pass unsaid.

LEAVING CWM

Each new step, a step away from Cwm.
The valley, our house, and the figure of mam.
I see slate roofs, smiling wet at the summer sun,
Tethered to the clouds, by ropes of smoke.

Half way now, I straddle the mountain pass,
The right angle of the gallows bows its head,
The Cwm is almost gone, sinking with each step,
The spikey Brecon Beacons, the winberries, bracken and sheep.

And yet I'm not alone, as running from behind,
A girl in a hurry, breathless and speechless.
Oh Marion, why did you have to come?
Dragging behind you, all I drowned seconds before.

"I came past the gallows, with their haunting hinges,
To tell how your dad was betrayed.
Day upon day the guilt has weighed me down,
I promised on my life, I would never tell.

One night a policeman came up our steps,
He asked to see our cellar, I hid the key,
But he wouldn't go away, so I gave it to him.
The door was opened, so to my first taste of fear.

Down the steps went he, in the lamp his eyes shone.
Picking out the condemming gleaming white fleeces and
The spinning wheel, mam froze me with a look,
Lest one breath, would break her into fragments.

He read his sentence, as the sheep-thief he charged her,
And dragged her to the door, then I think I must have screamed,
I shouted your dad's name, and where he'd find the bones,
And how my mam was innocent, I couldn't see him take her.

He straightened his coat, and buttoned up his book,
And said for a favour he'd see her go free.
They went up to the bedroom and locked the door,
The bed squeaked for ages, then after he just went.

I saw him going down the steps, then heading for your house.
Smart and smug and self assured,
Like a mated bed-bug.
Lowly and loathed, he took the guilt from our house".

Her eyes dropped, mine too, both lost -
In twisted fate and time, wrung out by our maker,
Or so the Preacher said. Then I couldn't help but notice,
How pretty were the plaits that surrounded her head.

I turned to Llangynidr, and she to Cwm again,
The drover's track seemed smoother, now I could trust again.
For every day I'd searched each face, for a guilty look,
But now I knew that it had flown from number four to eight.

AUNT NANCY

Nancy's full of talk and tea,
Lace and rounded as a pea.
She hurried through the purple hall,
To the parlour and Uncle Paul.

Uncle Paul lean as an aspen tree,
Tapped his pipe upon his knee.
Nancy quick as a flash,
Caught the falling ash.

THE SKINNER'S MATE

A new job, a new day, sitting behind a trotting bay,
"Yes Mr. Owen, no Mr. Owen, but it smells Mr. Owen"
From farm to farm barks the alarm, skinner of no charm.
Dead for days the tanner pays, feeds the carcase to the strays.
But God the smell, trails behind us well, like a snail's shell.
Good bye black-face, hello space, and a red frosted face.

SUNDAY TRIP HOME

Walking backwards up the drover's track,
Knowing full well, behind me looms my Cwm.
Looking through my legs it's acquired a lake,
With white puffy islands drifting in and out.

I think I am a boy again,
I can laugh run and play,
And see the funny side,
The stiffness of the mine is away.

Cobblers Lane, The Drovers then our steps.
Catch me mam, can't you see I'm flying.
Does she see how I've grown?
Pity dad's not home to see.

45

So time passes smoothly
Months and even years,
Twelve today and no fears.

CHRISTMAS EVE

Christmas Eve Aunty Nancy waves me off.
Snow lightly settles on the frozen puddles.
Drovers are few tonight, scarce another light.

By the steepness I'm nearing the pass,
But God, a light waves near the gallows,
What if it were a hanging night?

I take to the bog and skirt a wide path.
It moves too low and free for a hanged man,
Looks like a child, a girl to me.

Feeling a fool, I retrace my boggy path,
And strut fearlessly towards the light.
"David" I hear Marion's soft tentative call.

She'd dared the night to meet me here,
I bet her mother does not know.
But what a welcome, she is to me.

CHRISTMAS EVE   PART TWO

THE HAUNTING

Have you ever felt an oddness in a night,
Felt behind all solid things hides a hideous sight.
Seen the stars move around,
The occasional tremor of the ground?

Sounds leap out and bark, a touch on your back,
Or a shadow flits across an open track,
And all your nerves rush into a ball,
That rolls wildly towards a wall.

Bells and birds, whining winds, a hoarse sheep,
Even Marion's hand can't stop my leap.
I must run from the gallows-squeaking,
That seems to be walking, behind us creaking.

The house, the steps, my front door,
Quick, before the gallow clinches its jaw.
I drag Marion along behind, through the gate,
Slam the door just in time, the shadows now abate.

Have you ever felt an oddness in a night?
I see two seats, an old familiar sight.
Like,
Boots on the hob for the morning, reflecting
The dying light. . . . . . .

Is it tears of wild nightmares or dreams,
That pour down my face in streams?
I must be dead or going mad -
For there sits my Dad.

He was deported, but rescued by five men,
They pardoned him and sent him home again.
Boots on the hob for the morning,
Dad's and mine.

EPILOGUE

Now snow adds its cap to the valley,
Worn askew by the tilted terrace.
The seconds melt into midnight,
So too, the base of fire warmed chimneys.

The Chapel has sucked all souls in,
To curse and cleanse, then spit them out.
But purified by their singing, not sin
They burst out through the Chapel doors.

The procession peels off left and right,
Cold, like the sheepdog sees them off.
Bang, bang, bang-bang-bang.
Shut the cold out, and the Christmas in.

47

But wait, at number four and eight,
Parlour lights still faintly burn.
Two friends linger, and dare a kiss,
Then dash up their steps, bang, bang.

Derelict Landscape

The rock that has broken and toppled across the track
Where cattlemen drove their herds will never be moved.

The manners of the old men coming in from the fields
At nightfall are sweeter than the bodies of the young.

Diving for Sea Snakes off the Swain Reefs

We go down in clear water, in wet suits,
among squid and eels, stingrays—
jewelled reef fish in dense, rainbowed clusters. The snakes
come toward us, weaving anxiously,
mustard-yellow skin,
five and six feet long. We go for them
with our snake sticks, aluminium rods with
moveable jaws, grabbing them
before they strike and do us in. Lidless eyes that
never close, and flattened, rudderlike tails—
they move in, then twist away
resisting capture.

Topside, we take venom samples
from the fangs, harvesting the poison
they sent us out to find. We tag the snakes
and save a few in tanks,

the rest go overboard. They breathe air at the surface,
stay under for two hours.

When they bite, there is no pain. The legs stiffen,
the jaws lock. There's no known antitoxin.
Convulsions set in, and then
a failure in the lungs. The snakes close in,
under and around us, curling about our arms
and legs. We hold them off
with our sticks. They come in anger and concern,
eager for the kill, their hard magnetic eyes
drawing us back again, and back again,
until we're done.

Eden

I

BEFORE THE FALL

One day was like another
as they explored the Garden
and each other, their skin
sweet to the touch. Spiders
and scorpions ran lightly
over their feet; bees
gladly yielded honey
to the curious pair.

        They played
leapfrog with spotted beasts,
gathered watercress
from a brook, skipped stones
across its surface,
drank plovers' eggs
from the shell. Fireflies
lit their way at night,
blinking like erratic stars.
Heads pillowed on the animals'
soft flanks, Adam's and Eve's

sleep was deep and dreamless.

An infinity
of fruits was theirs
for the sampling but a cloud
spread across Eve's happiness.
She yearned for something
that would set her teeth on edge.
The one tree beckoned, the one
prohibition gnawed: a worm
at the core of her contentment.
And all the while, the red sphere
burned in the tree's green heart.

II

THE FALL

Eve was a little bird
hypnotized by the serpent's
sinuous glide. She bit
into the apple's heart; the tart
juice ran down her chin.

For an endless
instant, a great light dazzled her.
Birdsongs swelled till they
were deafening; her narrow world
expanded. She saw beyond
mountains and seas: a dizzying
glimpse of unimagined splendors.

She foresaw, too,
exile, suffering, pestilence
and war. None of them
shocked her like knowledge
of her own mortality.

Eve looked at Adam:
something was missing from his eyes.
She couldn't wait to share
her vision. Adam held back;
already he had felt the stirring

of a strange emotion when the snake
wound its coils familiarly
around his consort's waist.

But she insisted:
whatever the punishment, she thought it
a fair price to pay for revelation.
Her hand trembling, she held out
the fruit, toothmarks visible
on the red skin. Adam, who had never
refused Eve anything, bowed
to her blandishments and fell.

III

AFTER THE FALL

A chill wind swept the garden:
a few leaves fell. The animals
knew hunger for the first time.
The Tree continued to bear fruit,
unquestioning.

The snake, not one
to waste an apple, took a bite
and found he had no feet. Birds,
pecking at windfalls, suddenly wished
for words to put to their songs.

One taste,
and the iguana avoided its reflection.
Sheep nibbled on cores but were too stupid
to learn; the apes needed nothing
to hone their wits. A wolf foresaw
well-fed descendants lying by the fire,
never having to work.

Out in the world,
Adam blamed Eve for his blisters,
his painful back, the babies bawling
underfoot. Her quick retort:
Would you have wanted
to stay ignorant all your life?

Ephraim Destiny's
Perfectly Utter Darkness

(i)

I scalped a lie
       the other day
whooping outrageously
         it came
from the prairie,
      I toppled it,
pinned it,
  ripped off its warpaint,
& finished it off.
      Then I went on
to the next town
      Doomsburg,
        in the territory,
& set up my wagon
      next to the bank.

Folks,
  the truth of the matter is
a salve exists
      against the future
& I have found it!
      Now, I'm a boaster
but you'll acknowledge
      there's four parts
to truth.
      One of them's honesty,
another's a lie.
      As to the other parts
I might get to that.
        Frankly,
I could never pretend
    to be something other'n
what I pretend to be:
      a truth-telling man.
So let me sell you
     Destiny's Oil;
a fabled rub.

Apply *légèrement*
to the skin
          my friends,
them bad incidents
          'll glance right off you.
All you have to do
                    is pass
the E. Destiny test
                    for survivors
first.

Is there anyone here
                    who does not doubt
the future's a lot of
                    nonsense?
far too much
                    fuss made about it,
act with contempt,
          but don't let it
sneak up behind ya
                    with a pistol?
Marshal! I can see
                    you're just the man
for this doomy town!

And is there anyone here
                    looked himself over
this morning
          in the mirror
being the next
                    maybe
to have to
          press a woman
close
   & be
a bridegroom
          in his
too, too
   shining heart?
Young man!
          a splash of this
'll ward off any
                    folk discrepancies

53

a-coming between
    you & yr lust!

And is there a fellow who
                can ride
that desert there,
             who can brave
the tanglesnakes & witchweed
              on a moonlit night
by silence,
          who can look at
the horizon
       & let it
enter in his eye,
           so
he keeps that straightness in his trot!
You sir!
Look like an ostler to me,
          good liveryman
I'll be bound,
       & a man who
understands a horse's gait.
      I declare
this oil
    was made for you!

Lastly,
    I want a man
who knows about land.
               A man
who can look
   at the bend in a river,
look
   at a clump of trees
or a fine vista
       of the best grass
& ask himself:
     "Does not a man
become his acreage?
      Is not possession then,
a mark of time's propriety?"
              Concluding:

"Acquisition makes
        the fullest man
a pleasure to himself."
Aha!
I see the man
        to whom my neat address
has captured
        something of his star!
May I presume
        to tempt you
with this offer
        of my preparation—
all four upstanding gentlemen?—
        Step this way,
up on the wagon
        of my Medicine Show!
For being deft
        at knowing who you are,
I'll give you each
        gratuitous,
my bottled hope!
        Thank you, Sirs!
And now . . .
        Gentlemen . . . Ladies . . . ?
Would anybody
        like to try . . . ?
Ah yes.
    Good.
        Good.
Hand them down,
        Liza,
fifty cents a bottle,
        's what I like to see.
(*Get four*
        of yr prominent people
up on the wagon,
        appeal
with silky speech,
        a touch
of something intellectual,
        & all the rest
will buy
        yr merchandise
without a thought.)

Look at me with yr fingers, Liza,
in this darkness of our wagon,
                    I am yr calculatrice,
the mesh of yr doubtful, innocent pleasure
                            in which
what wriggles & kicks with triumph,
                        with bliss,
is finally caught. And yet, though
                    I have taught you
much, it is
            yr awakening that delights me.
Come to my side.
I have things to explain
which the darkness always
                more conduces to.
An irony that pleases me in this:
                        we are sentient
with the darkness
                numb about our faces,
yet later all the darkness
                be inside us
while the sentient prowl outside.
Let me cup yr breasts with
                my dry hand.
Yr eyes are like pale stones
                I once saw
staring from a clear pool
                & could not find again.
In the darkness yr hair
                is a noiseless fall of water.
I can feel it running off you
                like a map.
I believe
I am precious to you
                for the passage I give
from that unknowing life
                in your eyes
to this place of knowledge
                here. You wish to know,
what we most want,
                all, in our different ways,

from the passionate darkness.
                         Dear Liza,
because the Indian cut out
                    yr tongue,
because you cannot speak,
                         because
yr mouth is an empty
                    directionless fountain,
you have to trust my language
                    to give the blackness shape.
Look at me again
                    with yr fingers.
I'm a young man,
                    dealing in time.
With vigour left in me
                    I can teach you
how to remain
                    priceless, female, captive.
Read with yr fingers
                    what time has dealt you:
an old man,
                    a stacked deck of cards;
yr bearded mountebank

yr wise crook & lover

yr own rage

magnified.

          (iii)

What is the secret
                    that everybody knows
but don't know he knows
                    & therefore cannot tell?

An old Injun asked me that one,
                              folks,
& told me
                    how to reach the answer.
First find a pony that has wings,
                              he said

57

    & leap a bottomless crevasse.
                        Beyond, said he,
you'll see a desert
               wider than an ocean.
Sail across it,
            you will come
upon a lady Goddess
                whose female part
is bigger than a catacomb;
             she cannot find a lover.
Satisfy the lady,
            you will satisfy yourself,
he said,
    & gave his Injun look.
Now how was he to know
               I'd modesty enough
to know I couldn't do it
             & sufficient vanity
to take that challenge on?
               Four parts
I said there was to Truth,
           & vanity & modesty
the other two.
             If you think about it,
vanity & lies
             's what gets you
going in a
         good direction;
modesty & honesty
              the pair
that makes a good direction
            look right dubious.
Put'm all together,
            you get me. Well,
I took my catapult
           to scare off fiends,
& gave my pony
            green-leaf herb
that set his heart
          to battering.
He couldn't keep still, so
              together we
just ran for the ravine
               my little

intoxicated Pegasus
                  & me.
We floated out magnificently
                      on the air,
I had time to see
            the river
sparkling below.
                  What a jump that was!
My pony came down
              & gathered his legs
for the landing,
                came to a stop
& his heart failed.
                  He died under me.
I saw no desert.
                I had no boat.
I didn't know what to do.
                It was silent country
with an edge to it somewhere,
                so, on principle,
I walked along
              until a strip of sand
appeared. It went
              all the way to the sky.
There were ships out there,
                    marooned,
with skellingtons
              a-clinging to
their look-out lofts
              & a great tide of heat
came rolling to the shore.
                You could feel
the droplets on yr cheek.
                My eyes
were burning
              just from looking at it.
The light was clear as bone,
              the spray had whipped it clean.
I had no boat
              but Pegasus
& so I skinned him,
              set his rib-cage in the sun,
& bound the frame
              with plants & vines,

made him into
                a real tidy little skiff.
All I needed now to sail him on
                        was water!
By chance,
        looking up at me
from fifteen feet
                below,
staring curiously,
            white looking out of black,
a bit hungry,
        a bit creepy,
was my face.
                Perfect black water,
with my face in it
                & nearly
ten miles across
            to the other side.
There's one thing
            you have to know.
If an Injun,
        if any man,
sets you a riddle, a test,
            it's got to be possible.
No one imagines
            the impossible, that's
impossible. So,
            I looked down at what I stood on.
It was a boulder,
            much rounder & bigger
than the daylight shadow
            of the moon up there;
a cyclops of a boulder.
            It must have weighed
ten thousand tons, yet
            I could move it
with my little finger!
                One pivot
it rested on,
        all those days & nights
simply sitting there
            waiting for a push.
& behind it,
        all pent up

the part that held my searching face:
                              a lake.
I dropped my skiff
          into that black, black water,
& gave
      the rock
              a prod.
It rolled away
                  downhill, towards
the desert
              & ten miles of water
came after it.
              Can you imagine
how I rode that deluge
              making a first river
through the dreadful sand?
                          Fish jumped.
They dried in the air
              so fast, they popped open
like pea-pods
              showering seed from
their gullet, everywhere,
                              which
the water drenched
                  & nourished. Say,
as I cruised
              on the neck of the water
all around me
              trees sprang up,
& grass, & the most
                  reasonable flowers.
My pony boat
              flew through the desert
like it flew through the air,
                      till I landed
in cooler country
              on the far side,
& turned to watch
                  the glimmering scales
of that lake
              swirl, settle & sink,
leaving a green tail
              to grieve over flatland,
& pure moist air,

to pass like triumph
into my blood, a real
                    lung-herb.
It made of me
            a truly passionate man.
I looked for woman
            & there she was:
an Injun maiden
            big as a house,
squatting on a mountain,
                    legs apart
& naked enough
            to scare ya.
I could have walked
            inside her
standing upright.
            She
wouldn't have noticed.
                    Passion
was not going to be
            enough,
it needed thinking
            to augment it.
I took my
        little pony-boat
apart
    & cut some teeth
into a rib.
        Now I had a tool
to saw down
        two hundred trees,
laying each one
            lengthwise
on the one below.
            You'll appreciate,
I was on a slope, facing
        that open-legged beauty
                    & she
just looked the other way
                all the while.
At the finish
            I was standing
on a mighty pile
            of trees—

the biggest penis,
            gentlemen,
in the history
            of sex relations!-
with eight logs
            transversal
at the bottom
            to make wheels.
I had to smooth it
            if I weren't to
hurt the lady, so
            I used
the jawbone of my pony
            as a plane,
took off
      splinters,
squeezed
      the pith of gum trees
along its length,
            released
the stones
            that chocked me, &
started
      slowly rolling downward.
Myself,
      I crouched behind
like Hector
            in his chariot.
And do you know
            what that perverse maiden
did,
      gentlemen?
She turned on
            her tummy
& presented me
            her *cul*
            (as the French would say)
which was bigger
            than *Notre Dame*
in french France
            itself.
But I had my catapult
            in hand
& stung

63

            her tawny cheeks
with quick
            projectiles.
She gave a grunt,
                lifted up her body
& received me in
                between
those fancy gates,
                my whole forward being
& me,
        up to the swell of the root.
And by God, gentlemen,
                        she gave
such a squeal
            of pleasure
that a thousand
                watery lakes
& a dozen
            lively thunders
& the plentiful silence
                    of the forest
& twenty-four
                great rains
& the green, green acres
            of the prairie,
them grumpy hills
                & mountains
with their peaks
                in ice,
& the red dryness
                of the desert,
the whole suffering body
                of this continent
& the natural sky
                that looks down upon it
made a cycle
            of one year
in the space of all
        her satisfaction.
A pleasurable story,
                friends,
is the end
        which asks for more
but knows

                    there is no more.
                              Ah yes.
And the secret
            that everyone knows
but cannot tell?
            Later,
she told me,
            whispering,
in case
      she deafened me.
"Take off yr
            white beard, Eph,
pull in yr belly,
            straighten yr back!
You can never die
                  if you know
yr youth
      is always in you
& you can
      find it, touch it,
& release
      its energy
if you will
      only understand
the tale yr life has told
                  till now."
A blasted
            Injun trick, it is,
to set you
      a whale of a problem
& a crazy woman
                  to answer it:
difficulties being
            what the Injun mind
conceives
      as helpfulness. Thus
by brooding on the puzzle
                  you discover what
you know already,
                        &
by perilous adventures
                        come
to just the answer

you'd have given
if you'd
        stayed at home. I
didn't learn a thing
            from that maiden
I did not know
            before. Nor
did you.
        This youthful
body
    you see
is merely
        the body of an old man
on a constructed stage,
                        or,
to put it
        differently:
this old body
            you see
is merely
        a young man pretending
not to be himself.
                    Here
is what Time
            can really do.
It can make
            my body straight
make my voice
            strong & clear
comb the white
            from my beard
smooth my skin
            make my eyes white
make these
            cracked forgeries
of teeth
        white, so
you ask yourself
                if this
is Old Eph?
            or is it
somewhere else
            you saw him?
                    Ha!

66

Will you not
          good people
of this young town
               buy my products
& stay that way?
               Believe me,
that what you do
          is blessed
by what
     you've understood
of what
     I've had to say?
Let me sell you
          Destiny's Potions
The Finest Wares
     for a Complete Rejuvenation
The Best Nostrum
          Money Can Buy!

          (iv)

How d'you find me tonight, Liza?
          I find you perfect.
Am I old tonight, or young?
          You have lots of disguises.
D'you like me when I am canny, eh?
          Yes.
     Or like sagebrush?
          Yes.
     Or poison sumac?
          I do not waver
An when I become a mountain wolf, Liza?
          I must lie perfectly still
     Or a snake?
          I must be grass
     Or a fast pony?
          Drum me with yr heels.
Suppose me a mountain eagle, Liza?
          I am in yr talons.
          I soar.
I find you repressed,
          squeamish,
               flat,
                    passive.

67

Yes.
If I became a
            savage cougar
                    what then?
                    Darkness is home to a wild creature.
Do I never make you afraid?
            I trust you in survival.
Or make you weep?
            My weeping gives pleasure.
Or speak?
                    In my arms you
                        have learned what
                            I wish you to say.

        (v)

I'd like you all
                to take a look
at this here
                artefact.
a wheel
        of destiny
old Eph has built
                    to bring you,
each of you,
                immortal truth.
See how
        finely carpentered it is.
This wheel can spin
                    an hour
on just one push,
                & folks,
it's truly tuned to turn
                according to yr shove.
Watch it spin awhile
                    a-gathering
yr destiny
            into itself
& sleep
        beside the legend
of the Book of Truth.
                    Now

what's that boys?
                    A note of unbelief,
that low chatter?
Could I mislead fine intellectuals
                              like you?
I mean or say
                no disrespect
to yr religion,
                that's
a faith I hold myself.
                    But this
is Science.
          See
my secretary here, Liza,
                    a handsome gel.
Make a fine wife
            someone;
she's no tongue.
                Beautiful
she is,
      can't answer back.
                  Eh, boys?
From you she needs
                  a date of birth.
Can you remember
                  back that far?
And then if you
              will step
into the delightful darkness
                  of my wagon here,
with her,
        who has nice, cool hands
& a way
      of smilin' at ya
so she may weigh
                  a strand of hair
& place
        a gob of spit from you
in this
      old foggy vial,
& have a coin of yrs,
                  well finger-rubbed,
that she

may hold up
to this candle-powered
                    magnifier,
you'll come to know
                how you may feel
de rerum naturibus
                    irrevocable, strong!
& have decisions
                    take themselves
lightly
      as spring showers,
tho
   they mean risk
& maybe
        outward exposure.
Hey!
   If you would quit
shaking my wagon
                        I have a
real important question
                    all of you
should hearken to.
                    Aint you
inclined to hear
            a tongueless woman speak?
That philosophical experience
                            is yrs
for just one dollar.
                    And you
for such a price
                will then be sure
of being sure.
                The world could seem
a more considerable place
                        to those
who know
        how it will run.
Gentlemen!
Have I done something
                that would anger you?
Old feller like me.
                    A few tales.
A little colourful

        introduction to
philosophy. Surely
           there aint nothin in that
to make a cowboy whoop,
              is there?
Boys!
I have electricity back there
            in jars!
That's
    combustible potentiality!
What's that you say?
You want Liza?
She's no
      marriageable piece.
She's been misused
         by Injuns!
You'll turn the wagon over!
             Alright.
Alright, Liza.
         You better step down.
Take that young man
          there
as yr protector,
         show him
a favour.
      This crowd
has had its brains
          stampeded.
No, Liza, no.
        Don't look back.
Learn quickly:
    A soul can be made from grief.

    (vi)

In the darkness
        Liza
I imagine you
        still here.
           Perfectly
utter
   darkness.
I can slide my hand
         along yr flank

& seem to feel
                  yr quick breath
on my face.
It was a forced marriage
                  I know
& I know you did it
                  to save my neck.
There are moments
                  when you feel
you'd rather
                  have let the bad things
run their course.
                  Now
I'm on the prairie,
                  our prairie Liza,
listening to those braves
                  a-scuffling
round my horses.
                  Aint no good
to them Indians,
                  my horses.
They couldn't gallop
                  for a nosebag
of river-grass. Just
                  steady horizon-pullers.
So long as those Indians
                  don't get to thinking
they might *eat* my horses
                  I'll be fine.
But you'll
                  be getting married,
& I think to myself:
                  "Eph,
where is yr
                  natural-born wit
to take someone
                  like that
into a town
                  that aint got
hardly a single woman
                  & let her strut
that shapely form
                  of hers

up on the board!"
                    Well,
how was I to know
                    they had no women,
that no woman
                    would stay
in that town
                    longer'n she needed
to make herself
                    look real ugly
& catch
        the next vee-hicule
out of town?
                    And this
darkness won't
                    let me see myself.
I know there's
                    a moon
above this canvas,
                    veined pearl,
like a look
        of yr skin,
but yr absence
                    is all I can see
alongside me. O
                    I could go East
looking
        for another Liza.
Do Lizas
        grow on trees?
A forest like that
                    could extinguish me!
I've the grace to think
                    you had
a feeling for me.
                    Didn't I
make you see
                    a lot of worlds
that aren't real?
                    And
I never knew
                    whether you thought
I was real.

                    I know I never
looked real,
                being all my life
a kind of
        actor-man,
life just a play
            I wrote for myself,
see,
I know I'm a fraud,
                    Liza,
but I know my fraud
                    's the Truth.
Aint that truer
                than those
that pretend no fraud,
                call themselves
right serious?
                But frauds
do nothing
            in this life, Liza.
They don't advance
                    civilisation
not one jot,
            but sit
right clever
            where it's got up to.
No great will
            in them, Liza,
to take this heavy life
                    elsewhere—
they're too full of it;
                too much
of knowing what's what
                    makes them
a spectacle.
            The world at least
can be entertained.
                It's empty
& needs
        a human joke now & then
to remind it
            how serious
humanity can be.

You're

married to them

    Liza,

those empty, serious folk.

        They have desires.

They'll burn down

      the city,

stone a few

     citizens maybe,

hang some others,

       torture more;

they got *ideas,*

      unfortunately,

that won't let them

      rest.

They'll make a war,

      spread facts

in a kind of plague.

       The world is

what is said to be:

     "going to prosper"—

tho that aint for me, Liza,

       I can't prosper

in a world that thinks

       it prospers.

That

   aint my style.

I aint got

   no style. I've

no Liza.

   People

are fine

   but I've a

holy objection

     to them, Liza,

to the way they

     choose to live.

And now

   I'm a snake again

naked

   on these sheets.

I'm wriggling
            to yr cool boulder
hoping to hear
            that gentle
throat-murmur
            of yrs.
The blackness
            is brilliant
like a day
        in the desert.
I can see
        everything so clearly.
I'm going
        to make the effort
to speak
    from darkness.
Do you believe
            in messages
that can pass
            in vibrations
of light?
        What will happen
if I touch you
            with my thought
where you are lying
                silent
by the side
            of someone else?
What will happen then,
                    eh?

You know something?

I'm gonna try.

Fading Away

"A veteran of the Battle of the Somme in the 1914-18
War died from his wounds on Sunday. An inquest
verdict. . . . . .recorded that he died 'a victim of the
King's enemies'".
The Times, 3rd Dec. 1981.

Half a man, left over from some war,
Was pushed about our village in a cart
When I was young. Sometimes on summer days
They left him in the shade at the field's edge
Where we played cricket. Once a well-hit ball
Rolled to his wheel and I, retrieving it,
Came closer to him than I ever did
And saw the empty trousers folded back
Pinned to his crotch, and one sleeve hanging limp,
The good arm raised shielding his head,
White hand splayed, palm out, vainly fending.
He saw me looking and said "Bugger off",
The first time I'd been sworn at. After that
Lads good with the bat tried to reach the cart
Off every loose ball.
          When we were of age
To use the pub we'd sometimes see him sitting
In the Snug, propped in his cart, not speaking
Much, watching the cribbage players and the darts.
'Poor Dick', they called him and he gave his name
To 'Poor Dick's Alice' and to 'Poor Dick's Tom',
Though who they were I did never get clear.
It was said he had a couple of rows of medals
He wouldn't wear even on Armistice Day
When all we Scouts paraded, proud, in Church:
He didn't go, not then or any time.

It's years since I even gave a thought to him,
'Poor Dick'. He likely dead now I suppose
Along with Tom and Alice: and the cart
Is rotting in some shed.
          That "Bugger off",
Said softly, almost whispered, puzzled me
That afternoon. I could not understand

The cold eyes and the quiet, bitter voice.
I'd only glanced, not even at him really
But at the place where parts of him had been
Before whatever it was blew him apart
Out there, on some obscenely gallant slope.

Family Tree

They walked down from the mountains, north of Laz
The tall cheesemakers with their flocks of wives.
Sometimes they stopped to sell their milk,
Or buy a goat or girl
For yet another son.
They unbound bits of cloth to pay the tolls,
They slept in drafty khans, or on the hills
Whose humble yellow flowers made them ache
But they pushed on. At Turkish villages
They broke the bread, not knowing any words.
Then the roads grew wider
Or the shade of trees more feathered -
The distant domes were gold.
They entered Sham by an ancient gate,
They found a courtyard and they built eight rooms,
They tiled them with the blue of their Black Sea.
They planted lemon, and they filled the marble basin
With the butchered lamb. They bought the grain and oil
And they were home.

These were my father's fathers. Their white beards stayed
As fierce as mountain snow. They were as handsome
As they were unkind. Their daughters all committed suicide.

Fanciers

Tough men with crude speech
make nests of gentle hands
to hold their favourite pigeons
displaying them proudly, shyly.

Such birds cup themselves,
all soft curve, jewel eyes flashing
(above scars tattooed by coal-dust),
tilt iridescent collars to the light.

They come home out of the sky:
imagination racing to earth
flashing from grey clouds to strike
joy into quiet men standing by lofts.

Endurance flies muted colours,
freedom checked by that call
to come home, a helpless longing;
paradox beats out of each basket.

Their release is like love:
a pent holding in the warm dark
until this great swirl of seed
flowers the sky in giant umbels.

This flight, this freedom of air
spirals higher & higher — a way out,
an intuition, for men who tunnel slowly
through black rock, far underground.

They root each flowering fancy
here, between slag-heaps in Yorkshire
raising rare blooms: pied, chequered, barred;
wingbeats return round upon round of applause.

Father's Shoes

My father's shoes are by the hearth today,
Wearing his expression,
Seeming more himself than he
Since yesterday,
When he stepped out of them for good;
The uppers creased by his attitudes and standpoint,
His character ingrained on each
In profile, right and left.
Brown shoes. And donkey-rides ago
I breasted dunes of carpet,
Finding elephants on the Savannah—
Grey flannelled legs - my father's, wearing brogues,
Encountered at ground level.
So infancy returns in seconds
On its hands and knees,
His shoes, as then, like giant-killers
Filling the room—the beanstalk his absence,
Growing through the roof.

The leather has outlasted him,
Destined for Age Concern, his shoes,
Though he for ashes to ashes—
And someone, somewhere, burns alive
On the cautionary nursery page,
Leaving just a pair of boots
Upright in the cinders.
So father's shoes remain, alone in dust,
Forlorn and standing in for him,
Refusing to succumb to mortality,
Withdrawing now into a cardboard snapshot album
And a spot below a tree
Where he grows out of them, smiling ahead,
Trapped in the Brownie Box.

The leaves are curling
And he is turning yellow already.
Seen from the wrong end of a toy telescope,
Who would be in his shoes?
Already I cannot touch him through his distance glasses—
Yet he has only just started his journey.

Few And Far Between

If only we could forgive ourselves, and didn't
have to have somebody else forgive us—

Where I came from everybody could see anyone coming,
even storms: and out there the etiquette

was not to say right off what you came for when you did
or ask anybody why, if they came where you were

in all that space, and time; it made for a kind
of trust, or—well, it was like trust.

I remember some of those storms, how the dust
would kick up before them in the wild wind, and behind it

the blueblack cloud piled high white on top
with lightning flaring inside, and maybe only a few miles wide,

coming over the desert sort of slow and grand:
you could have got out of the way if you wanted to

but nobody did: as I said, seldom enough is welcome.
Didn't I say that? One night when Mother was away

my dad and I followed a storm clear down
to Needles in the state car. His job

was to take care of the highway so it was work, sort of,
for us to ride along behind that cloud we could see by its own light

through the wild fragrance the desert has after a rain
in the lone car on the road that night, to keep track

of the damage it did. He showed me a place near Essex
where a flash flood had ripped out three hundred feet of roadbed

two years before, where it hadn't rained
in fifty years before that. The foreman said so,

Billy Nielson, who had lived there fifty years
without seeing the ground wet.

My dad and I stopped on the grade below Goffs
and watched the storm go on out of his territory

across the river into Arizona
where the sky was getting gray,

and turned for home as the sun rose behind us
back across the clean desert in slant light

that lit the smoke trees in washes that were churned smooth
where the water went, and sharpened along the edges

through Essex and Cadiz Summit, great tamarisked Chambless,
Ludlow for breakfast with the humorous Chinaman, Lee,

Newberry Springs, Daggett and Elephant Butte, Nebo hidden by wire,
on home over the hill to Barstow on the good road.

First Fish

I showed my wife my scraped thumbs
    that held open the bass's mouth by the teeth.
Later, she said
I looked radiant.

The teeth were tiny, a little longer
    than the whorls of my thumbprints are deep.
Holding the fish
in the dusk, I looked happy,

she said, for the first time in months.
    By the dead tree out of the water, near the leaning wall
of the living trees,
the bass was the one thing

that was radiant, more alive than the skin
    of my hands, than my blood feeding mosquitoes,
though I know
I was happier.

I squirmed in the boat, so
    full of myself, crying out to her on the bank
where I thought she
cried back.

She walked down from the lit house as I
    walked up with the jaws held open. Which light
I looked radiant by,
I can't say.

By garage light I pried the rubber worm's hook
    from the throat, noticed the green scales, the naked
gills parted like bracelets
around no wrist,

like broken rings of a planet. I put it back
    in the pond, an act I wanted her to see
and note the significance of,
as much as myself.

The fish leaned first left, then right, loose
    in my hands, and I thought in the dark I would
see its belly
up turn, pale.

Then it fled, and my wife was with others,
    playing cards, happy, she told them, that I
was happy, radiant
for the first time. . . . .

For a focus like that, for a still point,
    though the fish fought, for a day dividing all days,
I had forced
myself forward.

That evening when our host took me out
    and taught me to snap the line near the banks
where bass fed,
what you knew, my wife,

I can't say. Just as which day ahead
    will be happiest, best, I can't tell.
But I knew
I would catch that fish.

Flower of Spring

With the breath of a new-born babe
A benison falls on this house.
In the small white room
Lie mother and child.

It will never again be the same
In this place of wattle and daub,
Under the aching ageing beams
Lies the flower of spring.

As years pass, as saplings grow,
Sounds in the panelled rooms
Will change with the ebb and flow,
With life and death.

But the benison from a baby's breath
Is in every part of the house
Where in the small white room
Lie mother and child of spring.

Flowered Apron

Although radishes were always much
        too strong, I grabbed
a bunch to take along and tossed my suitcase
        in the car. My father used to kid
that radishes were Mother's "favorite fruit."
        When he'd been there the two of us
teamed up, teased her.
        I gnawed a radish, let it crisp my teeth
and numb my tongue — as if it made me know
        her better — now that she was needing
me. From my fern porch, the road would lead two hundred
        miles to her slim bed — now solemn with "the tied-down
sheets," a nurse said on the phone. I drove too fast —
        inside the gap of wind and raced against the furrow

of a storm, where rain turned grass to gullies,
        swallowed into rivers. Clouds stampeded
hard across the fields of Illinois where half
        the world's corn bread was growing.
Wide wind pushed my car, bent back a small bird's wings
        and caught it struggling like a stroke inside the sky.

The sun — and calm soup-kettle ponds, vanilla
        smell of fields, and locusts humming like machines
that milled the wheat. The radio played madrigals
        of forests and ripe clover, but the road
was long — until the night turned silk with city lights,
        and I was there. Yet not.

She mumbled, "No, that's not my little girl,"
        and turned away. Like summer wind, her hair
frayed out across her pillow. Words rolled round
        inside her head, her eyes were skating
circles. Or perhaps she looked out at the moon,
        cocked like a rocket in the pines
and ready to go off through heavens, as she mined
        her head for words to tell herself
that she was still alive. She spoke
        as if a priest had pressed a wafer
to her tongue. "Dearie, you came!" she said.
        "She's always cresting on a flood of facts,"
my father used to tell me, frowning some,
        "and yet that bright head never drowns in them."
Now all she needed was a seldom word
        bobbed up and watery as communion
wine, the splash of each one new upon her lips,
        sweet lick to taste.

At her apartment I tried on her flowered apron, crisp
        as ruffled curtains. When I phoned long-distance-
cousins, I could hear her voice echo
        my own — my mother stuck inside my head,
glued tight. Then later, as the crickets rocked the night
        to sleep on rusty springs, I thought
how long she'd waited for her turn —
        her being first and most important, calling
all the apples in our family tree to come, those apples
        rolling down into her flowered apron, home.

Following Cows Through Ash

Following cows
through the village of Ash
on a bright October morning,
I see where the truth lies.

The massive, flat hips
like plateaux above cliffs
sway with the gradual earthquake
        of their walk.

They are old women
who should wear black dresses
and black shawls, to go regularly
        to mass, to mumble.

The sun is in front of them.
They are a deep forest against it,
dark thunderstorms of heavy flesh
        against the light.

Their udders are weighted
with the labour of the cud
and the mansions of the chirping
        cricket.

Walking in their wake, in cool
sun, clear as a miracle, the cowman
taps a hazel switch against his boot and
        they know what this augurs.

The cows edge round a parked van.
One snuffles at the wheels and ambles
onward, ignorant in the rain-washed day
        and the village street.

Then - one stops, turns its head,
watches me in my car. Its ears are up,
its eyes as placid as love. It has an idea
        about me I cannot touch.

Another, pausing to think again
its dream of nothing, tugs hard at lavender
bushing over stones: a twig, softly, shoves
        its head aside. It lows.

And that is all. Cows. The sharp light
of the last of summer's dance. Their graceful
bulks. Nuts firming in the trees. Truth coming
        as easily as milk.

For Dolores

Sometimes I'm one man who knows
where he's come from and what he wants
— something different from other men —
like a particular raindrop in a storm
destined to fall on a certain spot

But in the company of millions
I easily forget myself
remembering rain as a whole rush of love
from the sky to the earth, and I confuse
even upwards or downwards in my flight

Now I also know that it is sensible
to give meanings to things, to talk of clouds
and condensation, to make deserts fruitful,
yet sometimes even in the company of millions
we can't make sense out of the weather

Mostly I am content to make my own decisions
following some old paths and making new ones
yet again I am a jungle of people
I am everyone in this prison and those who put us here
I'm a family at dinnertable and a starving child alone

I am waiting though I have no time to waste
every moment is precious when there is nothing to be done

like a bird hovering over many resting places
or a speck of the abandoned sea hardening to salt
turning under the sun to catch the light

One of these millions that I am
takes delight in making you
into more people than I have in me
knowing that when you leave me you come back to yourself
a secret flame, warming and stirring
the many winds I am that move you.

Belfast Prison, March '71

Going Blind

What happens is that one eye loses interest.
His children's faces look like painted plates.
His wife walks into the wallpaper, and the cat
Disappears completely.
He doesn't tell anyone. He doesn't complain.
He calls it his bad eye and gets used to it.
The other eye sees better than before.
Nothing is difficult.

When he sees nothing with the eye, he closes it
To try the childhood trick of seeing shapes
Behind shut lids. Still there.
A candle in the window, lightning over water.
His talent is for special effects.
He quits his job and seldom leaves the house.
The good eye shifts to heroic scale.

Each day he wakes to catch a different scene.
The patterns are landscapes, unpeopled and remote,
Places he has never seen. These are the hills of Samarkand,
He thinks, the Costa Brava, Patagonia.
There is so much to see.
He can easily ignore three whiskers, thick as broomsticks,
And his own life-sized reflection in the closing,
Green ellipse pleading, "Feed me. Feed me."

Grimes Graves

The diatoms are lying in their vault.
Their number is without number;
It is beyond thought.
They are incredible white tons
Of chalk.

Down go the miners through the grass
Into the calcareous tree.
They take a fragile light and pass
Amongst imaginary
Branches, finding stones like glass.

They think that they are farmers,
Not miners. And only by
Their arts
Of sacrifice acquire
From selfish gods incessant harvests.

Or so their bones would indicate.
Whatever fears
They had are finished with. We are too late
By several thousand years
To meet them and can only speculate.

For instance, just today I find
A poet, unsuspecting,
Is a miner too — a kind
Of casual pitman
In the undefined.

One day when he is lean
He finds a space
He can enlarge. When it is smooth and clean
What he has found will fill a place
Inside a magazine.

But really he has queered
It for himself.
He heard
How on the shelf
A poem dies. And it is as he feared.

The stones that undergo
Their necessary change
To what we know
Are altered like his thoughts, becoming strange
And different from what he'd hoped to show.

He will not quit. In short, it is his art
To know the floorstone and the shadow
Ultimately yield a part
Containing the familiar rainbow
In its heart.

And there is something like it here.
Though almost infinitely rare,
Each word said underground still, year
By year, assumes the wheat stems and the air,
Becoming as we listen clearer,
And, on the wheat tips, clear.

Happiest Girl

Mrs. Mary Leighton's 89-year old body was as frail as a wigwam;
A house of bone she lived in, covered only by a stretch of skin
And a faint white dusting of talcum powder.
Somewhere in her body grew a rebellion of cells —
The ranks of mutiny silently waiting to erupt.
Oblivious, she laughed for me and said
"Ee, luv, I'm th' appiest girl in th' world!"
I was glad it was true.

And there I stood in my white coat and blue trousers[1],
Wanting to be a friend rather than an Efficiency —
I didn't want to Organize her.
How I wished I could banish her threat of pain
With pink carnations, or the sun, or a song,
As I watched her head with the old, old mist of hair around
And helped her climb the stairs towards home.

Beautiful, wonderful Mary!
(How my throat hurt as she patted my hand)
"What would I do without you?" she said, and laughed.
I tried to laugh too (if only from duty).
Only my white coat and blue trousers stopped me
From hugging her to me and crushing the cancer
And climbing each stair for her, taking her back
To her pink carnations.

She is the sun and a song and pink carnations.
She was the truth when she told me of luck and of fortune,
And of the happiest girl in the world.

[1. The uniform of a hospital physiotherapist.]

Horses Burning
Nonantum Hill, Boston

Come over and help us,
the words put into the mouth of an Indian on the official seal of the
Massachusetts Bay Colony. In 1664, at the time John Eliot
translated the Bible into the Indian language, there were several
hundred members of the Nonantum tribe; in 1823, none.

I
(Autumn 1944)

I hear them out of sleep,
no early cock of dawn,
but the horses, their death cries,
in the night, from the burning barns—
it was a war
the whole hill could hear.

Blackout—through the gap
in the green curtain we could see
the valley rank with fire.

91

Overhead, through red mist
a single searchlight mourned
the enemy who never came.

No blitz, neighbor—Peace,
whispered the warden at the door;
this disaster is—natural.
Civil, we drew lines
of water, ferrying
the pitiable tin pails, hand to hand,

down to the hot barns where
the horses screamed air,
the fire in its own voice
cracked and spit terror;
and I learned a word, DEAD,
what the black headlines had cried.

I lifted the cold tin
almost too heavy for a man;
and my taut muscles spoke
that natural ache of pity,
what we were crying for,
the horses, ourselves, and the war.

Out from that house of fire,
through beamed black crosses, the sorrel
stallion leapt, limped free;
thick legs stopped in quicksand:
corpse for the catkins, sacrifice
to the final silence.

And in that fiery silence
no water shall ever quench
rose in their bones the Nonantum
to claim their stolen home;
astride their ghostly stallions,
they rode the white night down.

Beat tnem down, beat them down,
and under concrete stifle their cries.
We assigned to the flame
the last farm of Boston,

Indian seed, corn—our home
is nowhere: the city on the hill.

The black firemen, like priests,
moved through the stinking night,
dragging their coiled hoses,
but the water fell short.
Too late, they brought the hand-pumps,
from the country towns, fifty mile.

From Strongs Brook
the great arcs of water
steamed to the crashed timbers.
It was finished now. In the false dawn,
the black beams stood like mourners
and we turned, empty, back.

Above the smouldering ashes
of barn, horses, and hay,
good Doctor John Eliot,
Bible in his savage hand,
proclaimed our Christian Commonwealth,
in blood, on the Indian land.

Down at Black Market,
Butcher Black worked late:
tomorrow, bring your dollars
for the secret ration of beef—
and what they would never admit
the good hill-people ate.

                    II
              (Winter 1944)

But the children spat it out.
We gathered in the woods on the hill
and breaking bamboo stalks for spears
searched out the Indians we knew hid there
and on our way killed the black snakes,
stoppered the tunnels of the moles,

and with bits of glass in the sun
startled the ants at their entrances

93

and at the pit of darkness
called out the great bear who lived there:
When he roared, we ran,
abandoning our long spears to him.

At night we burned the grasses
and called to the Indians to come back.
They would not. We had seen them ride from the barns.
We built a pyre of pine for them
and pissed our homage to their god of fire—
they would not come back to us.

III
(Spring 1945)

O lost tribe of Nonantum,
if I held my ear to the grass
I could hear you walking in the earth,
in the long rooms of death;
and once, something like a voice
cried out your garbled curse.

Walking back alone,
up hill by the last Indian path,
I stepped on a pheasant in his starting-hole—
the feathers, the white ring shot through me—
the bells of my bones rang out,
woke me from that sleep of reason.

I shut tight my eyes: the rings, the rings
of Saturn rushed towards me
gusting me up to galaxies,
to that arrogance of imagination
where I ride in the comet's eye.
Beat them down, beat them down.

In their black business suits,
the puritan elders whispered,
Come over and help us—
They cut down the pine and the catkin
and over the farm they built of crushed stones
rows of boxes for the pitiless men.

IV
(Summer 1980)

Nothing remembered—in the lots and lanes,
the inhabitants of these model houses
dare not honour the sacred bones;
but, underground, there are lost rivers,
suburbs of uncivil animals
who wait there, who will come back.

And when we go down to our sleep,
what disturbs us in the hollow night
is a taste of burning, of blood,
something animal, earth,
come to disrupt our concrete patterns,
something un-American, something which will endure.

The child I was
speaks to me out of the charred grass:
Are you crying? Yes—for the ghosts
of horses, and for the lost caves of the past,
and for the future, lest it see
butchers inherit our history.

Hwa and History

'Flat-faced Hwa,
how dim you are!'

they laugh
they call her names

'Retarded,'
the staff remark

at whatever point
you may locate her
on the syllabus
she'll still be in the doldrums

Vietnamese Hwa

her history teacher
who's giving them a test
about the Vikings
next Thursday
is trying to explain how
more than a thousand years ago
Eirik the Red's son
Leif the Lucky
stumbled on America —

but it's Hwa's pudgy hand
'Please, Teacher, what *ago*?'

we laugh
we call her names

because ago
is the blitzfeuds
that wrenched whole families
up by the roots
thrashing them out of their world-tree
to be wave-people

it is the old pagan sap
beginning to rise
and beat out
Lindisfarne, Sutton Hoo

ago is runes on standing-stones
dragonships in burial-mounds

and not
(where history
stops for Hwa)

Vietnam
nine years ago
when the bombs
decided on her home

In Honor of Roaches

Man is by rights a higher being
But I'm one who can't get used to seeing
The results of my bug-spray genocide

Their limbs so decently tucked in
No malice in their form or face
It eases my conscience that one decides
On a dish for his final resting place

Clean china, white: in no way narrow
The spirit of this little hero
Who chose the funeral of a Pharoah

"Small Beowulf," the dragon sighed
"The honor is all with those who died."
And though I'll have to wash the plate
I don't regret that you lie in state

In Memory of George Seferis

Angelic and black, light . . .
Angelic and black, day . . .

Black is the light behind the blaze of day,
your summons comes, clear from the angel's throat.
The sun's dark horses call your heart away.

Though bright the strain of dawn upon the bay
which in celestial ink its author wrote,
black is the light behind the blaze of day.

Though morning's cloudy mares are dappled grey
with rainbow mane and many coloured coat,
the sun's dark horses call your heart away.

Their riders gallop by. Too swiftly they
will trample down the shades noon kept afloat.
Black is the light behind the blaze of day.

Night's chariot approaches. Don't delay.
Haul evening's golden gate up, cross the moat.
The sun's dark horses call your heart away.

You scent that whinnying wind? The horses neigh.
You see it now? You hear that perfect note?
Black is the light behind the blaze of day.
The sun's dark horses call your heart away.

Katrina Changing

from Vermeer's Kitchen maid

Do you still see a calm
contained kitchen-maid
pouring cool milk
from a pitcher
with just the right glaze?

I am Katrina,
frozen in a false moment,
that single respite
in a back-splitting day.

After the long haul
from the well,
the yard clearing,
the bread is now baked,
the milk settling,
next the coals for the foot-warmer,
then the continuous service
unrolls again.

Have you just walked in from the street?
I know the squatters have been evicted
that someone is shooting at the police
that an overturned streetcar is burning.

Look at me carefully.
At any moment I may use my girth.
I am getting strong enough
to hurl this pitcher out of its frame,
spilling milk onto your clean tiled floor.

Kite Aiyo

The Savannah simplified
the segregation of tribes
into Woodbrook, Maraval,
Belmont, Laventille
as we simplified into one,
sitting on that hill,
the tribe of children.

Seen from the high altar of Lady Chancellor,
beyond the genuflexion of trees
in their soutane of leaves
Port of Spain sat
like a congregation sleeping under hats
of corrugated eaves.
Who could tell we knew,
in that smart girl's offering,
a beheaded coconut, chaliced dew,
blood of the sun's first bleeding,
a stained glass window, the sea,
that the sea gull's scream
was the future?

From our hill the Savannah seemed
below the sea.
The boys conduct a symphony

of quavering kites
that variegate the sky
bobbing and weaving
like fishes fuguing in a reef of colour.
They float with long tails
hanging like notes
on the shifting surfaces
of lined horizons.
And then one straight-pitched, a plunge
as vertical as the stem of a treble clef,
and quick as a sword fish lunged
"Kite aiyo!"
I saw that kite base cleffing away
the long langorous wave of the tail
a hundred handkerchiefs from a ship's rail.

Still as a painting on glass
the red sea parts
slit by the zwill
of a ship's prow.
The steamer, Moses, farts
farewell with a rusty blast
like an old woman at early mass.
And I will leave you green
my brown sapodilla
as surely as the red sun
leaves the silvering sea.

Later we reminisce.

We were not enslaved
by
"Capitalism and Slavery".
In imagination
there was no boundary
to be
beyond.
These were to come,
later,
we were still young..

And then I watched
poets going to lunch

on the hearts of children
and livers of drunks.
It was in England
that I became
West Indian
from books.

You never left
what I longed for,
with a pastoral longing,
the simple pleasure
of spreading toes
sucked
by yielding lips
of mud.
Thank God, but
what of
Mona
with its Rasta,
grubs and gowns
and sandalled frowns.
Shit!
or metaphysics?
Doctah.

We envy
the Keskidee
discuss
the hibiscus
and give the Cascadoo
its due.
But coat of arms done drawn
Scarlet Ibis beat unicorn
UN representative sworn
Consitution reform.
Students in satin
asking serious question
in Latin
"Quis custodiet
ipsos custodes?"

Lion

1

Lion came down, a goldrush, like the sun
Clearing the steps of its throne in a single bound
Acknowledging his lord, the man
Was taken on the instant, against such skyfall
He hadn't an earthly, nor had the woman, no

No, she pleaded, no, but the swallowed man
Answering her cry, spoke with the voice of Lion
And his heart, even as it went out to her, had become
The hungry heart of Lion, there was nothing he could do

> She heard Lion's world-eclipsing roar
> Shatter the mountains

> And the horizons were altered

> And the stars re-tuned

2

When he had eaten, Lion lay down in the sun

The man and the woman climbed to the lids of his windows
And peered out

An unexplored expanse of grass and dunes
Floated their gaze out over the edge of the world

To the invisible kingdom

They were in a right sphinx, Lion blinked them down
Gently, into his furnace

3

While Lion was sleeping, the woman crept out of his mouth
And wandered about in the darkness
Weeping
For her lost life, and the several things
That had fallen out of her handbag during the struggle
Like her mind, her heart, her will
Her self

And the man came out also
In search of her, meaning to comfort her

But Lion had modified their eyes, and all they saw
Were the shadow-jackals that slunk between the trees
With eyes the colour of accusation, lust
Remorse, and worse

Lion woke, sprang
Claimed his own with a roar, and the scavengers fled
This time the man and woman were glad to be Lion
To be safe inside, to feel the power and grace
Of Lion in their limbs, for their flesh to flow like gold

Again Lion slept, and again
The woman crept out and the man came after
But outside Lion there was nowhere they could go
No-one
They could be

Lion had become their death-in-life, their life-in-death

And nothing would ever be the same again

4

Unable to hide from Lion, they tried to tame him
They mobbed him with garlands and gibes
Called his bluff, gave him pet names
As though they were free to bring him to heel
And dismiss him when they were done

But like a kitten among moths, Lion batted down
Their flimsy resolutions to twitch in the dust
His pupils magnified the sun, under his dreamy gaze
Each loud declaration of independence
Shrivelled to a whisper

> The woman murmured in Lion's ear
> Angel or beast, said she
> Go back, go back to your heavenly lair
> And then I shall go free
>
> But her eyes said, Stay for ever, let
> This story never be told
> And the hands that she wrung were the same that clung
> And clung to the mane of gold

Lions

Although you meet a lion in unlikely places
he's seldom dangerous:

a shaggy flower, its coat full of bloom,
an old gentleman with an untidy mane who knew your grandmother;

a dirty boy squeezing his tail between his legs;
a policeman glittering behind the leaves, surveying his kingdom;

the bird puffing out his chest
to sing ferociously outside your window: I'm hungry.

The roar of lions is well-known,
also their silence.

When they walk slowly in the opposite direction it's a challenge
like girls that stare at you over their shoulders.

They pace backwards and forwards like worried housewives
or it may be a sign of boredom.

One season crouches
and leaps suddenly onto another.

104

Without turning toward the lawn
I remember the fear,

the silence of sleep in the jungle.
I taste the spilt blood.

Growl of thunder
changes into purr of rain,

evasive mist
into conspicuous snow.

Old, shivering as I stare out the window
I keep telling myself

in midwinter in a country without lions
I've seen their footprints.

Looking after someone else's bathtime child,
Lithe and wet he becomes physically shy,
Covering his seedling groin as if in play:
I smile and retreat tactfully so he may
Wash in private. But when I go to find out
How he's doing he has fled to some hide-out
All his own—though it is not at all the same
If the adult refuses to play the game.
When after half an hour he isn't bored
I look under beds, where toys are stored
In cupboards, behind settees and under stairs.
At last I find him playing behind my chair
With the youngest erection I have ever seen.
Surprised, I do not ask how long he's been
There. I want to know if, that young, it satisfies.
I'd ask a friend but they may well lie
Either way. Later in provocatively
Torn pyjamas he asks me to count the
Age-lines of a dismembered tree, now a
Bannister polished smooth by his trousers.
My face is close enough to the concentration of his
That I find I am waiting for the soft-focus kiss.

Lower Lumb Mill

*for the teachers and pupils of Nicholls
Ardwick School, Manchester, who spent a
week writing at Lumb Bank.*

Here are the reins of
the work horse, the traces
of water in harness,

still handstitched in stone:
and not slack, though water
falls in idleness, though weather

buffs and beeches the black
of the chimney that once blackened
the beeches; and still rises

out of all proportion
to rocks and stones and trees,
a first draught, a delineation

of valleys since transfigured
by cubes and planes and cones,
a shadow of Hell or Halifax,

of mills and manufactories
wherever water ran,
terracings and resurfacings

worn through again as the work
moves away. Now tree shadows
box the walls. Green thoughts

wash at the drystone. Or
under the petrodollar's
green shade, green thoughts

walk down from Lumb Bank. Between
anorak and wellingtons, jay's
wingflashes of tight sateen

as the walking disco, Angela,
Jennifer, Beverley and Mo,
sends a green bluebeat through

the thoughtful thrush-tap on stone
of the geologist's hammer
Mohammed would like to have,

and stirs Farah's tree of silence,,
just broken into the first leaf
of her sketchbook. Our other lives

star the valley, the Persephone
in each of us given five days
above ground. Half in thoughts, slim chances

huddle at the valley's rim,
wind-silvered underleaves,
the ghosts of our fits and starts.

'Where to go from here?'
A rainflash of fieldfares turns
into dust shaken from a duster.

Out of memory a ring-dove calls,
Darby, be true, Darby. . . .
And truly, where can we go?

Even as we ask, a road
finds our feet. Gently down,
under moss'd tree roots,

between banks of primroses.
Sunlight mullioned through branches.
Madrigals of blackbird and thrush.

Now the hill is a honeycomb
of lanes we wander two by two,
in conspiracies of reverence,

little arches of whispering heads.
Each couple through its kissing gate
threads onto a village green

107

the generations in their loveknots
have stitched as white as the may.
Here is a month of Sundays.

Afternoon is a tune
from Elgar, on which the sun,
in a setting by Vaughan Williams,

never sets. Elms constable
the high clouds. Yews cloister
the path. Lawns are palladian

with light and dark. We walk
under great protections,
into wise enclosures.

Distantly, distinctly,
as clear as the voice of Clare,
a yellowhammer sings,

*A little bit of bread
and no cheese. A little bit
of bread and no cheese.*

The lawns spin like roulette wheels.
Cloud smokes in a ring. Towers of
coin rise on fields of baize.

The Trade Winds blow us back
to our places. Angela? Mo?
Unheard of. Battened under hatches,

Bristol fashion. Ship's ballast
to the Indies, or King
Cotton's fields. Mohammed?

Locked in a Kipling ballad
—one of many who move
between the lines, and serve

the twenty six soldiers
of lead, appearing only
as points of silence.

As for me, who should I be
but Hodge? The original blot
on the landscape, the labourer

beyond the ha-ha, who trespasses
twice a year on the park
of English poetry, the blackface

morrising and mumming
through the gates. Clodhopper.
Clown. Brother to the ox.

(the opening sections of a work in progress)

Me Nans Song

*Ellen Avis was born in London in 1884
and died in 1969 aged 85.*

1
Forf sun two yeers no more
A child were Tomas
When e wer taken Brian
Brian Brian Boru
Me sun me babe so sad
Bu nour Ive yew
Brian Brian Brian Boru
A long times gorne
An nowh Im owld
An in me grave Ill soon be cowld
But Brian Brian Brian Boru
Tomas nour is surely yew
As Ive gorne owld wiv memeries
That sturs in the fire

An murmers in me ed
Bu Tomas nour no more is ded
Brian Brian Brian Boru
I awlwus ad a soft spot for yew.

2

I ad a dreem
A pennys worf I fort
Nuffin bu a childoods dreem
Bu the loosing of it
Broke me bleedin art
So long gorne
So long gorne
A dreem of tuppence
Bu I ad a penny see
A dreem of tuppence
But ownly a penny see
Me farver e wos ard
An times wer ruf
We awl wor boots
Bu we never ad enuf
To buy me tha tuppeny dreem
So long gorne
So long gorne.

3

Yerv got the cheek er Charlie Bogey
Brian Boru
I wudnt put up wiv cheek like that
From anywon bu yew
Yer makes me lose me temper
An I knows that its qwik
But yerv got the cheek er Charlie Bogey
Nour dont yer try tha trik
Corse it dont wurk on me
I wos owld afore yew wos born
So dont yer cum it wiv me
Corse I dont lik it see
Jus yew keep quiete
Nour dont seys a wurd
Corse yor me faverite
A little white bird

Fly aways Peter
Fly aways Paul
Bu stay wiv me Brian
Brian Boru
Corse yor me faverite
Me suger on bread
Yor me Tomas from eaven
Cum bak from the ded.

4
Ard yer ad to be ard
In Blackfriers
In nineteen undred
I wer sixteen yeers owld
Wiv me long blak air
An awty wiv it
I didnt av a care
But yer ad to be ard
We wurked in the dustyards
Me muvver an me
Sortin ouwt the rubbish
Larf yer ad to larf
Fit enuf to shit yerself
An swear
I didnt av a care
Bu I wos ard
Lorst in awl that dirt
I fink I lorst me yoof
Me childood perished
Under me awty nose
An in the muck o London
I surched for it for days
An then I fowned it
A rose
A wivered in its dyin
An ardened in the cowld
Of nineteen undred
Wen I wer sixteen yeers old.

5
Granfarver looks at the picturs
E cant read the print
An theres the wireless

An the Trocadeerer
Wen wer not skint
E gets in for sixpence
I gives im a bob
An e brings me bak jujus
No I aint gort one nour
Id give yer one if I ad one Brian Boru
Ard gums me faverites
An lockjaw to
Why dont I get fawse ones
Lik yer muvvers yew mean
Becorse I dont want to
Its as simple as that
Yor awlwus arskin qwestuns
Nour go owht an play
Dont look so urt
Yer can stay if yer want to
Werv blowters for tea
Of corse therve got there eds on
I cooks em for the cat
Bu storp askin qwestuns
Corse I dont ave the pacience see
To arnser polite like
Thats the way it is wiv me
So dont tak it to art like
Corse I dont meen it see.

6
Im appy its oppin
Me oppin box packed
An wer leavin tomorrer
Nowhr go tell Big Pat
To set er clok urly
An not to be late
Else were go wivout er
Bu I fink we might wait
At least for a minet
Peraps for a few
Bu tell er be urly
An Kafleen to
Corse Morgs booked the lorry
Sharp at eight
An yer knows shes no pacence

Yer know she cant wait
Wiv Lally do lally
An pissin er draws
So tell em be urly
An not to be late.

7

Me farvers sister Jude
Died on a ot July
As ot as ell it wur
Tha July
She wer browt ome in er coffin
To lie in our frunt room
An we awl sat there waitin
Wiv faces long as doom
As ot as ell it wos
An us in our long blak froks
An such a stink there wos
Lik shit an owld mens socks
But strange an new
An wen we fowned out wot it wos
Wot a to do
It wos er that ley in er coffin
Swelled she wos wiv gas
An gettin bigger qwicker
Fit to fart an bust er gut
So we gets the undertaker
To screw er coffin shut
We buried er next mornin
An we awl cried there an bak
Ot as ell it were in them carriges
Wiv us awl wraped in black.

8

Wen yer go dahn oppin
Knok at number one
Then yerl see our Lally
Wipin er fat bum
Wiv an ee i o
Ee i o ee i ee i o

Our Lallys a do lally
Do lally in er ed
Aint got no sense nor knowin
Do lally in er ed

Wiv an ee i o
Ee i o ee i ee i o

Bu Lally likes er oppin
An picks ops wiv the best
Dont yew mind er larfin
Dressed only in er vest
Wiv an ee i o
Ee i o ee i ee i o

Mad Lally feches warter
An logs an faggets to
An she luvs me Mog er muvver
An likes er Irish stoo
Wiv an ee i o
Ee i o ee i ee i o

Our Lallys a do lally
Do lally awl er life
Bu dont yew mind er Sunny Jim
Unless shes gort a nife
Wiv an ee i o
Ee i o ee i ee i o.

9
I likes a drorp of brandy
Wen Ive go a bob or two
Bu I dont drink beer not ever
Like sum women do
Not beer not me not never
An I never smokes a fag
It just aint done in my yung days
An as for takin snuff
It terns yer nose awl snotty
Lik that owld snuffy Kate
Er that cawls ere uninvited
Wiv the snuff awl up er nowse
But I likes a drorp of brandy
Wen Im owt on Fridy night
Awl dressed up in me best
Me best blak silwk
An garters
As green as Irelands grass

114

An if I as to many
I fawls upon me arse
An neer dies larfin in the Val
Wiv sawdust for its grass
An spittoons for its piss pots
Bu I dont drink beer not ever
Now dont yu bleedin larf.

10
Yer granfarver fownd it in Flanders
In the first great war
Shatterd it wer awl muddy
An lyin awn the floor
E fort it might be silver
It aint bu I kept it see
Corse a cruficicks for ever
Keep it now for me
Awl the bludy mud of Flanders
I worshed from orf its face
I polished it awl shiny
Yer culdnt find a trace
Exept if yew look closer
There from eye to cheek
A crak or tear a fawlin
Nour dont it make yer weep
For awl that mud of Flanders
An awl that bleedin pain
As left its mark on Jesus
There so bleeding plain.

11
I dont want is pictur
Ung on the wawl
It only reminds me
An I aint gort no cawl
To daily remember
Them oos as gorne
Corse es livin inside me
Not stuk on that wawl
Es livin I swears it
Es part of me see
So I dont need no pictur
Makin me sad

It only reminds me
Wen realley Im glad
To be livin
Im glad to be ere
Alive wiv yer awl
So dont yer stik me
Up on that wawl
Wen Im long gorn
An lorst in me grave
Jus keep me insid yer
An dont yer be sad
Corse Im ere deep inside yer
Brian me lad.

12
Yew light the Christmas candel Carrie
Ive ad it blessed
An I gave the preest a shillin
I culdnt giv im less
I awlwus as it burnin
On the sidebord by the door
So yew light the candel Carrie
Like yer dun afore
An as its burnin
An spittin owt its prayer
I remember them thats gorne
An thems that are ere
So light the candel Carrie
An fank gawd for the year
Thats burning like me candel will
Me candel for the year.

13
Seventeen cum Sundy
Thats the number on ouhr door
Bu it wont be there Mundy
It wont be no more
Corse there pullin it dahn
Me Brian Boru
Corse its owld like yer nan is
Me Brian Boru
Seventeen cum Sundy
Its me faverite song

I sings it forever
Forever me song
Seventeen cum Sundy
They seys its a slum
But awl me life shines there
As bright as the sun
Seventeen cum Sundy
An its nineteen o one
Me lifes awl for livin
An mines just begun.

14
It aint the same as gas is
Theres no shaders on the wawl
Bu I meens to get used to it
In no time at awl
I likes me flat
Its neer yer mum
An neer the park
It warms me art
T see a bit o green
An if I cawls up
Carrie
As I passes by yer flat
Yerl ere me cawlin wont yer
Corse Im just acrorse the street
Me televishons dandy
I as it on sum nights
Bu thems thats inside it
Givs me a frite
Wot wiv awl there watchin me
I knows its not awlright
Yer sed its awl electrik
An just a macheen
An lik a magic lanten show
The bests thats ever been
But it aint the same as gas is
If yer knows wot I mean.

15
We wos browt up Cafolik
Strict
An me farver wos a man from Cork

117

E used a stick on us
Me an Dick an Jule
An the yungest Moggie
I ad to look after em awl
I wos the eldest see
Awles the eldess me
Nellie Jones thats me
Me muvver wos Welsh
Owld afor er time
Little she wos an nice
Not like farver wiv is cane
Eres a photer Brian Boru
Ive ad it seventy years
I dont look at it orften mind
Ive gort no time for teers
Melencoly thats wot it makes yer
Livin in the past
But then yew cums an wakes me
An we as a cup o tea
An I awlways enjoys it
Our cup of tea.

16
Scool wos diffrent in thcm days
Them times lorng ded
An sumtimes I rememburs
Wen Im lorst inside me ed
An I walks them owld scool corredoors
An plays in our bakyard
An seys yes mam to our teecher
Tha nun woo never smiled
Unless she spoke o Jesey
We used to drive er wild
The poor owld soul
She sed er usband in eaven
It puzled me for days
Me farver lived in London
E wos usband to is wife
So I arsked me teecher
Owtright in the clarss
If she ever visits eaven
To be wiv er owld man
An she smaked me bleedin arse

An sed Id be lorst forever
If I didnt mend me ways
I wos ownly eight
An I cried for bleedin days
Scools wer diffrent in them days
Nitty Nora used to cawl
Werd awl line up in summer
Inside the classroom all
An ave our air inspected
It werent arf a larf
An if we ad little lodjers
Werd aff to ave a barf
Bu awls thats wos is gorne
Like the shaders on the wawl
Yer sees em but yer cant tuch em
Or reed yer childoods scrawl
Thats writen in yer memries
That ornts yer as they cawl
From awls thats wos no more
Scools wos different in them days
Them times lorng dead
Bu sumtimes I remembers
Wen Im lorst inside me ed.

17
Times as gorne an lorst me
An I wanders in me ed
Cowntin awls thats is no more
An them thats ded
I sees em awl a smiling
Muvver farver
Moggie Jule
I ears em cawlin
Like fogorns in the pool
Of owld forg London
Me lifetimes scool
I ears em ows I ears em
Brian bright O Lyn
Theys cawlin times as short
As tuppence worf o gin
Its the landlord cawlin me
Time ladee if yew pleese
I larfs an nods an smiles an goes

I knows that I must leve
Bu yew go ome an ave yer tea
I opes its sumfing nice
Dont yew worry Brian me boy
About me
The nursus ere are good
As good as good can be
So yew go ome an ave yer tea.

Miss Williams and the Death-Watch Beetle

The death-watch beetle from the church
   Got into Miss Williams' head;
Flew from the church timbers
   And lived in her brain instead.

Tick, tick, tick went the beetle,
   At night it was very bad,
But even in the day time
   It drove Miss Williams mad.

And her pale blue eyes were haunted
   With the overwhelming fear
That as she stood in the village shop,
   Somebody might hear.

All through the winter nights and days
   The ticking never ceased,
And when May came with leaves and flowers
   The sound of it increased.

Miss Williams put on her grey straw hat
   To deaden the awful tick
And went along the sunken lane
   Where the buttercups grew thick.

They powdered her shoes with golden dust,
  The grasses waved to her knee.
The sun shone on her, guinea-gold—
  Miss Williams did not see.

When she reached the end of the sunken lane
  And came to the road beyond,
She crossed the road and opened the gate
  That led to the round field-pond.

Tick, tick, tick, went the beetle
  In poor Miss Williams' head;
As firmly she marched into the pond
  And lay down as if in her bed.

The duck-weed covered her pale blue eyes,
  Her hands were crossed on her breast;
The death-watch beetle flew back to the church
  And Miss Williams was at rest.

Monsoon

The sky overran me—no let me get it right—
bergs of clouds hurtled overhead like trucks,
panes of lightning hung till spilt by thunder,
the bowl of hills darkened and went under,
drowned in warm rain that swallowed all my light—

I ran for shelter to your stone flank,
rough as pumice, warm as polystyrene,
and still dry. All round the ground stank
and seethed: you lay crashed, immaculate, serene
despite one arched and bangled madder foot
broken off
and elsewhere—
I had photographed
its tasselled, bulging ankle beads before
but here—
impossible Goddess to get all thousand ton of you
in my Mamiya.

Deep forest light, the thrash of rain, high heaving trees
conspire to make me want to come,
to join your green cathedral's vast release—
no use. These cinammon curves of yours, made plum
by rain's long dagger stains, baffle by their size:
instead I huddle like a lamb, a foal, a son, and seek the calm
inside your waist's deep swerve. The rains rise
to new plateaux of intensity, splattering
thick as horse piss off your surfaces, shattering
me like rattan, neck and back—I run again,
camera cased in Snappies chromed in rain, bumping
my knees, ridiculous, asthmatic, hearth thumping
as I slip and stumble, splosh and lurch and slide
through this red soup along your swelling side—
to hide like a tick in your armpit recess
where the droppings have dried like sweat on a dress.

I watch the flood, deepening, drown your fingers.

An alien European thought occurs
to a mind swamped happily till now in Sri Lanka:
"How stupid to die five thousand feet high
Alone and unseen, how silly to drown,
just when at home I'm becoming well known,
corpse eaten by leeches and tropical creatures
and a paragraph in the Trinco Times
six lines long and my name spelt wrong,
will be all by way of an epitaph—
and even my wife will say he wasted his life—"

"But on the other hand," you said in a voice
like pythons cruising across wet leaves, as
the rain hushed all around us, "where better
to die, than by my still hillside,
my struggling, poor white lover?"

I had reached the shattered boulders of your shoulder.
Pale whips of bamboo grew in twos and threes through you,
long leaves quivering:
I watched my wet brown hand push them aside
—and looked straight into the curved house
of your face.
You lay upon your side,

the volupt cheeks, the open blind, bland eyes,
the jewelled and unaccusing brow,
the everted stone bow of your impossible
to Western senses mouth, drawn fatly vertical
and slightly back, the buddha smile
that maddens modern man,
its message: swim no more.

O petrified imperatrice you stun me
to a calm which copies yours—
the rain as cold as Russia now and you steaming under it—
a monkey scrambles screaming
up your neck, scampers teeth and arse away to launch
in a spread agony
of arms and legs for the nearest rainswayed tree—

"Surely" you cajole, "surely
you have some cream quantum
of yourself still left for me?"
Damn you - fuck you, I say. You smile.
I put my foot in your lips:
I hang on to your nose: I lever upwards
to your earlobed neck. I feel your smile
close round me as I climb:
I haul myself between your hut-sized breasts—
Green streams have dammed with leaves,
and you are slippery, emerald, algae-skinned.
On hands and knees I seek your navel
and in your girdled vulva
a whip-like snake lies curled
clasping and unclasping in a pool,
jade your dark stone, and garnet-eyed.
Head lifts: eye sights: tongue tastes:
body esses this way, that, to the pool lip—
a loose snake, mind, and me atop
the Goddess, on its patch—
the mind skids, spins, and with sickening slowness
dances slam into the wall—Reality occurs,
as glass and senses smash.

Behind me I felt your smile broaden.
A liquid not quite rain ran from one corner
of your peerless mouth.

123

In the end of course
the snake slid off one flank wriggling helplessly
while I fell down the other; him like an eel
me like a fool, and in the endless crash of rain,
I heard that smile of yours,
a voiced breath in the throat, an access
to the dream. Heard then gone.

When I flew over you later Goddess
with my long lens hanging out and down
like a donkey whopper from the chartered chopper
I got a better shot
of you, steaming in the morning mist
being picked over by monkeys:
it was printed in the magazine.
You were not there, but elsewhere,
in the warm and soaking earth,
and all I had was a shot of cracked and brownish rock:
no seed, no snake,
no smile.
We have escaped each other again Goddess
and the monsoon has gone to the North.

My Second marriage To My
First Husband

We married for acceptance: to stall the nagging
married friends who wanted us
to do it there and then—
with them. In the downy wedlocked bed
we ask "Is there life after
one-day honeymoons to Kissamee Springs?
Was I all right?" The answers, woefully,
are no and no. And yes,

we lollygagged down the aisle, vowed
to foresake dallying, shillyshallying and cleave

only onto one another, to forever romp
in the swampy rumpus
room of our eccentricities: that sanctum
sanctorum where I sport
bedsocks and never rise
till noon. What did we know?
Did you know my love for animals
has always been acute? Perhaps in time
I will become a shepherdess, a jockey.

At the reception every table was adorned
with toilet tissue cy-
cloned into swans. When I unraveled one
to find the charm, the management
was shocked. Dismembering swans!
No bride had ever. . .And the prize, a little gizzard
of a ring, was disappointing. Oh, Person,

was it worth it? Of course,
we fit at dinner parties. But as one part warbles
to be normal, another puts a spin on things.
I see you striving to frolic
in your steelmesh tweeds as I model
chiffon voluptuaries the colour of exhaust.

In the wedding album we end or commence
our revels. There we are! doing the cha-cha-cha
to the boom-chick-chick band
in our dyed-to-match togs.
We're getting fat
on the eats, foaming
white crumbs, "Honey" and "Dear"
cumbersome as live doves
on our tongues.

Bring squeezeboxes, gardenias,
a hybrid of the two. Congratulate us,
chums. Smile and freeze: our dimples
stiffen to resolute, framed stares. How adult
we look! Our eyes burn
stoplights in the instamatic squares.

Night Bus

You have to hold on to your faith in a world outside;
that, where the road bends here, the thin copse lifts
its fingers of trees in the dark, half shielding the field beyond
where three horses always graze, the two dappled, the one brown.

For no-one looks in at the window save your own ghost
keeping pace. You press your shoulder up against the darkness
that presses its shoulder up against the glass. There is nothing
to be seen past dried mud splashes like grey feathers.

And you know there could be anything out there: the bus
is lurching on a knife-edge ridge, precipices right and left;
or that you and your companions never left the garage
but wait in a windowless hangar with the engine revved.

Rx: Old Hotel Facing The Sea

Sated, wanderer fed up (for a while) with clamor,
shove in the city, I find you, keeping a steep
cliff seedy company, gardens a wrangle of weeds,
roses gone random, trees clutched by vines, stammer
of stones bird-ordure mottled, chairs reeds
(wicker) unravelling on the porch deep
shadows pattern as I come up to sign
the register for isolation's wine.

For almost no one's here, I note at dinner
surprisingly good. (Soup, lobster salad,
decent wine) served by a college boy
enthusiastically polite, winner,
he tells me, of two-mile track trophies. *Roy*
he grins introduction. His taut skin's a ballad
of suntan. Miraculous waves ridden, surf-
board his steed, unruly sea his turf.

But he carefully doesn't intrude. Someone's trained
him well. After shortcake I descend a windy
tangled way to the seafront, museum of wood
and shell art objects depths have generously rained
on sand I sit, staring. Cold. I could
say I've a cancer, growth beneath its rindy
cover proliferating. Nodules of Large Questions
have driven me here. I'm a colony of conjestions.

Gridlock. *What's Life about? What am I doing
on my pinhead portion of globe?* Last week a friend
(20) clawed breathless by real cancer, souls
wasted in war's spreading wastelands. I'm wooing
peace of *my* soul. It starts with one. Holes
burrowed by crabs fill with moon, portend
darkness moving towards light, stay the why
trembling all shine, the heart's disturbed sigh.

Moon in a hundred panes facing the sea.
One hundred rooms. How many lives? There
in a top floor eyrie I imagine a dance of bones
in past years, lovers free of Victorian tea
at Mama's garden reception at last. Moans
ache in the ear. They twist, believing fair
weather is lovers' due, forever. Forever
sands shift, forever ties relentlessly sever.

In a middle window, middle aged ennui. Distant,
he dresses for dinner, she powders a purposeless face.
In the Palm Court below, entwined they will separately dance,
separately die. Moons move on, persistent
offerings of light we *will* deny. Glance
at a ground floor pane. This is the familiar base
of an old woman, pockets empty of everything
but outgoing tides. I see her, her sad gas ring.

My hard bed. Ocean ceaselessly thudding.
Mind in sleep ceaselessly probing. . . .Breakfast
is gallant and savoury. Roy tells of a beachfire!
clams, marshmallows, laughter, his eyes relieving
a while my gloomy quizzical weather. . . .My attire
is swimsuit under a dress I doff. Overcast
skies clear. I dive, turn, turn
in exuberant blue under the eyes of a tern

I begin, shortly, to sketch. Or is it a gull?
Lesson to be learned. Look, only a spar,
or air, for holding. I lay down my brush, wander
dunes wild with grasses, holding. Hull
of a boat studded with barnacles, holding. I ponder
a pool left by the tide, holding. Far
back the beach, the old hostel, holding, a shell,
life gone, holding: light, sea-runes. In the ell

of the porch, later, I sip a passable gin.
Philosophy can be facile. Nothing's easily
come by; everything's easily lost. What,
then? Roy waves on his way to begin
dusk-surfing. Hope, holding. Beside me a pot
of primroses reaching towards light. An old man wheezily
sings in the vast, and empty, ballroom. I applaud
his mettlesome show. Laud, old man, laud.

Only a scant week here, or, a whole
week here. The point is viewpoint. So I am stretched
to believe in silences moving in webs of light
on early morning walks, in the sovereign roll
of sea. *In water life began.* White
on the swell, a sail, holding in wind. Etched
over char from the beachfire, elegant shadows of birds.
The climb is towards higher air. I hold those words.

On His Deathbed The Acrobat Tells His Daughter To Buy Land

I see now
it was never the sky
I wanted

though for years I perfected
leaps and dives, arching, curling
tucking my chin hard into my chest
to spin free
far above my shadow.

Now I see
it was always the earth
its mysterious pull
I was celebrating.
It was always to return
to the earth's hard bargain, on two feet
my arms spread like wings.

There are enough birds, Edith.
The air is full of seeds
far better than we can ever be—
invisible, merciful.
When I watched you pass the hat
I wanted to crawl into our wagon
and lie with my hands crossed over my chest.
I wanted to count the potatoes and flour
and find for once enough.
I wanted to melt my father's gold watch
and buy you a horse
and shoes of thin leather.

Remember I never asked you
to walk on your hands.
I respected your fear of heights,
of the fireworks we set off
at the end of the show.

The hard-packed earth at the center of town
where the people gathered
their thin shoulders touching,
that was my passion.

Remember before each trick
it was the red earth
I rubbed into my palms.

Parachute Music

"It isn't simply the wind whistling in your ears;
there is the helmet and the visor and the jump suit.
I wear my ski suit, the red one, and ski boots;
that way parachute music sounds hollow,
far away but not faint.
Far away inside my head, Babington.

You remember the sound De Gaulle would make,
like humming or clearing his throat,
before he began to sing La Marseillaise?

Last week they gave me a red smoke canister.
In my red suit, trailing red smoke,
I was a comet, Babington, a falling star.

But it is better without it, the smoke;
better when I leave no mark in the sky
and think of nothing else all the way down
but myself in space. Then parachute music
ends in a gasp of arrival
and the creation of the world."

Physiology

They brought her their frogs to kill.
And she would hold
Each one
Struggling a little, in a gentle hand.

It was not fun,
You understand,
Just something which had to be done.

From mice (not nice!)
She would have run.

But frogs: ah, these
She loved, and so could kill
With ease.

Plato Decided Tennis Balls
Should Be White

Plato decided tennis balls should be white,
tennis a white ballet on a green lawn
figural as the chalk White Horse at Wantage.
Cricket and baseball should be pastoral,
the players should be spheres, rolling on felt,
clean as the white statues of the dead
that look their axial lines of recognition
six feet over our heads in the monumental
white city of Washington, the real
inhabitants of the perfect capital.
Snow falls on the grass. Form is killing.
Plato did not like optic yellow balls.
The white pavilion on the hill at Stowe
is empty except for our imaginings,
the snowman at the eighteenth green at Crewe
and the standing stone are broken from the ring,
and white bicycles drifting through Amsterdam
turn and fall like skeletons in the desert
next to the elegant camels and Mercedes.

Putting weight on. I can feel it settling
in all the wrong places. Any serious
reading nowadays and I end up afraid
for my eyes. But I creep out of bed, and sit
for hours in front of an unmade fire,
quietly getting it down on paper,
and no expense is spared; it comes cheap
at any price. That it comes at all
satisfies.

Writers (good ones)
are ridden ragged. (What exactly
is doing the riding is another story.)
They are piled up, layer on layer, and then
set alight (a more adequate figure). All
they were ever intended to do was blaze.
The few poor sticks of furniture might have been
home for someone . . .

            Hold out your hands
(the least you can do in return)! Shall we play
at transmitting the spark? Till the ends of your fingers
(Hold out your hands!) catch and flame—
if it smarts a little, for you too, all
well and good—like so many candles? Mm?

Rembrandt's Tobit

*a poem in eight sections based on
Rembrandt's depictions of scenes from
the Book of Tobit*

1   *Why**

He woke up in the morning blind.
A swallow shat in his old eyes
as he lay sleeping in his mind.
He almost lost that too before
he found his way in his own door
and sat, sure that he could not rise.

Between the window and the fire
he waited in an absent light
for his slow flicker to expire
and for Tobias to return.
And Anna watched him smoke and burn,
spinning their thread into the night.

It seems the purpose of the son
to find the fish (surprising key)
and with its gall get the work done;
to touch the old man and make sure
the love in and behind the cure
is strong enough to make him see.

*After the drawing *Tobit Asleep*, in the Museum
Boymans-van Beuningen, Rotterdam.

2   The Wheel*

Tobit would listen to her spin.
The click and whir, and her own hum
mixed with the wheel's, made sense to him.
And she would look out on the town
to tell him who went up and down.
The thread she spun would twist and come

fine, strong, the way he liked to feel
its purpose tense between his hands.
It gave him light, almost, the wheel.
He could imagine what she said
and give up wishing to be dead.
Tobias perhaps understands,

taking his worries to the loft
and wondering what he will do.
The slow fire with its crackle soft
speaks crumbling in his sleepy eyes.
Anna stays by it till it dies.
The story spins them swift and true.

*A composite of several depictions and imagination.

3   The Three of Them*

Arrested, Tobit clasps his hands.
Outside in some far land of light,
he knows, Tobias understands,
sure as the spinning wheel, what fire

133

draws them together, what desire
a son and father need to fight

the distance they require between:
and Tobit's own remembered road
spins out behind. What do they mean
to one another, these three fates?
Rembrandt in this case understates
how each, connected, shifts his load:

how Anna, spinning, waits in work
while her son, with the angel's aid,
cuts bravely, slowly, through the murk
that clouds his father's strong belief
into his own wife's house of grief,
and home. Three threads, a single braid.

*After the painting *Tobit and Anna Waiting,* in the
Museum van der Vorm, Rotterdam.

4   *The Fish**

Surprise! A magic fish takes shape
and leaps and snaps. Tobias shrinks.
The angel from his own escape
looks calmly on the nasty sign
and hands his friend a hook and line
(perhaps). The scene God makes and thinks

complete with cow and farmers deep
in view, cliffs rising fatal, sheer
above the mysteries that sleep
and wake in these slow distant trees:
this is the real scene Rembrandt sees
around Tobias' comic fear.

The River Tigris does not know
the story it has spawned and fed.
All miracles must somewhere grow
in the creator's fictive mind

as paths and rivers shift and wind.
Tobias went where he was led.

*After the drawing *Tobias Frightened by the Fish*, in
the Albertina, Vienna.

5   *Return**

There's something funny. Raphael
may not really be there at all.
But some guardian—who can tell?—
distracts Tobias on,
brings him the hope he finds in dawn
and leads him into night's long fall.

So very funny. Through those wings
some Rembrandt does not care to look.
Can Sarah see—as she bumps, sings
a donkeyriding marriage song—
certain as she rides along,
Tobias (as they cross the brook)

is her man? Tobias smiles.
This man with odd wings is sure.
This man lifts and reconciles
him to Fate, the journey home.
He does not return alone
but happily carries the cure.

*After the drawing *The Return of Tobias and Sarah*, in
a private collection, Newbury, Berkshire.

6   *Welcome**

The blind man in his ringing cave
gropes deeply for the hidden word
heard from the comfort of the grave.
So unfamiliar, gone so long.
The nearness of the spoken song
moves Tobit to the voice he heard.

135

The moment wavers at this crux,
Tobit still feeling for the door,
his trouble gathering from flux
to meet the embodiment of joy
in his miraculous dark boy.
Now as the heart of his slow sore

comes open in his hand and face,
he needs. That is the meaning here.
He does not reach for light or grace
but only for his only son;
and only when the way is won
will he look back and see it clear.

*After the etching *Tobit Moving to Welcome his Son,*

7   *Surgery**

The tense conjunction and its poise,
a magic distillate in time,
lives in that depth beyond the noise
of children playing in the sun.
Tobias has his growing done.
He bends now in his able prime,

the power gathered in his deft
and loving hands to sting the sight
back in those eyes. The warp and weft
of Tobit's memory will be
lit in the new way he can see.
Already something's coming bright:

long in that deep and lonely maze
with Anna's voice, with no dog's bark,
he nears the threshold of real days
again and feels the strange old sense
of light and color in suspense
waking in his frustrated dark.

*After the painting *Tobias Healing Tobit's Blindness,* in
the Staats-galerie, Stuttgart.

136

See how the angel lifts, and takes
a backward look at Sarah, leaves
with sudden glory. Silence breaks:
we hear the rush of Rembrandt's sound
dashing in his ears. On the ground
a family of faith conceives

power. And the angel knows
as they come to know him, *now.*
Raphael, companion, *goes*;
and following him with her eyes,
Sarah clasps hands; Tobit falls. Wise?
Who is wise? All wonder. How

does a winged angel look? Look!
Miracle! It was all real.
I vanish. See? Here in my book
you may keep my image, friend:
see, Tobias, how we end
and what divine wings we conceal.

*After the painting *The Angel Departs*, in the Louvre,
Paris.

Resurrection

Out of the eater something to eat,
Out of the strong something sweet.

(Samson's riddle for the
Philistines; Judges 14:14)

I
two seasons

A dead lion, bees nesting
among his ribs. Amber dripping
from white bone, amber sealed
in wax.

Honeybees have also nested
in a tree outside my window.

Sometimes they climb inside glass panes,
pace and wait on wood frames,
    their wings shiver and sustain
    a noise   a sound   a hum.

Insects create new words
in summer: they speak in Xhosa,
a language of clicks and whistles.

I watch them build their nest,
fortify it against the coming cold
with honey, their dead, and wax.

In the fall I watch them die,
thorax, abdomen, slowly working
beating a pulse without veins or blood.

Enough of empty shells rustling
echoes on the sill,

I leave when it is fall,
no longer stay at home nights
to watch them work

I make my paths through beds
of leaves and ash

walk down autumn streets
and when lights illumine leaves
I dream the yellows of the bees
    honey; dream the creamy white
of wax.

II

Voices   sounds   drums
awaken the dead.

138

Chainsaws with their sound
of a million hives
were made for this awakening,
this opening of a tomb.

Dig through leaves at the base
of a sycamore, sift loam,
lift stones; dirt cemented
by the blood of time and trees.

When the tree is wider than your arms
ask if there's some spirit
you should pray to before

you start the first cut,
horizontal; to show the tree
where to lay its bones

then to take the wedge;
diagonal cut from above
to just beyond the center

backcut; horizontal again,
the plane defined by the chainsaw's
blade, sawdust, smoke; your sweat
and the tree's sap.

All intent on two dimensions
the plane of the blade against the tree
for the final cut.

This sycamore was hollow;
at its center a skull, some teeth,
vertibrae, the bones of a coon
settled through the trunk
from his grave in the branches above.

I keep the skull and some of the bones,
glue the jaw together, the teeth
in their places. I call the skull

"Lazarus".

Last summer I sought out that tree
in six hundred acres of woodland,
found it   tapped it   played it
for a drum.

Put my voice inside
called, "Lazarus, come out"
put my hand inside, brought forth
bees and honey, pain and wax.

That night, with my hand wrapped
in linen, still swollen,
I dreamt the amber of bees
        honey; I dreamt the creamy white
of wax

the carcass of a lion
which gave shelter to a bee hive,

bones sleeping in a wooden tomb,
the rustling echo of a voice:

"Take the grave clothes off
and let him go."

Sad Companion

The sandwiches we hid inside the smoke-hole
for our years of long retreat, have disappeared.

Even when the sun blazed in like Heaven
through the eagle-port
above the hidden entrance to our cave,
the dark was full of inward shapes.

We banished Watty Maddock
for giggling as we chanted our sixteen pledges,
in code,
so Tom suggested we recruit the thoughtful cow,
wedged in the narrow part of Satan's Throat.

When we sang the song of welcome
it rolled its slow eyes at the flames.

Knives too blunt, we couldn't swap our blood,
so we singed the furtive symbol in our hair.
We tried to brand the cow,
but it sighed and ate the candle.

We vowed to share Mary Bullimore between us,

to send instructions to the starving poor,

to rescue spiders that crawled into our wax
though we'd give up
if more than three legs were pulled off,

and to find a sad companion for the cow.

But I don't trust Tommy any more.

On the day I came back early,
found him peeing on the everlasting flame,
he said the wind had spun him round
—but shadows didn't flicker on the stone,

and someone gave my trousers to the cow,

and in the playground Mary shouted 'Jerfal',
our third most secret word,
and everybody laughed,

and I found a spider with no legs on,
on the floor.

Shelter

The sun falls all afternoon, to earth,
Lands behind these spring elms, but can't hold
This precarious edge where they root—
Draws the elms with it, down into dark.

    At movies, Beth and I'd hold hands, palms
Sweating. We'd suck humongous red hots,
"Atomic Fireballs" — as, onscreen, Sarge
Flashed and swept whole nests of Japs, no sweat.

    Arms tight round each others waist, we'd weave
Home to Beth's, skip every crack—to save
Her father's back. He'd be standing watch
Against the window with his bottle.

    She sat next to me in school. We'd crawl
Under the same desk in the bomb drills.
Once Miss Cole wrenched us up, bawled us out
To the office. Beth's dad came down, blanched.

    He muttered what difference did it make
If we held hands at the final flash—
That week, backed the station wagon up,
Lugged rough two by fours and big gray blocks.

    With elm sticks we helped him dig all day,
Till our eyes met the earth's edge. He said
We were planting ourselves, roof of stars
Sprouting up from us here, our shelter.

    We dug our own hole back by the wood,
Built our shelter walls deep with his scraps,
Covered it with his old study door.
There I'd test the warm curve of Beth's thigh.

    He muttered if they just had let him
Fly by the stars, he'd have flown on by
The huddled, pinned lights of towns and dropped
Nothing, not the first light flashing out.

He stood watch at his whiskey, said stars
Grow up over towns, they'll never drop
The bomb, they won't bomb our street of elm,
They test it on far islands of palm.

Beth's hand warms my knuckles. We stand watch.
The elms will rise again with dawn, sun
Flash the earth's edge, climb to lose that edge
And shelter us with calm morning light.

She winces: in her, our child kicks, testing.
She smiles, reaches out to me, lips parted.

Sources

I come from a family of docile women,
unlined in age.
They bowed to their station
ever gentle, wise-eyed,
like Welsh goats which somehow they resembled.
Late, I saw my mother's face take on
gazing innocence of a scapegoat
when her fury had weakened.
She alone among the quiet women
raved and fought her fortune
till it was clear she was mad.

On the Bay of Conway sands
great-great-grandmother
lifted a conch instead of a ram's horn,
calling the children home.
They spoke a mysterious tongue,
passing the boundary into song
without volition or awareness of distinction.

Great-grandmother Williams had eleven,
she never murmured when her husband wandered.
He in no way broke the marriage bond—
just took a "walk-about" as the bushmen did, I've read.

Aunt Nellie and Aunt Bess continued
to live at Rose Cottage, mildly moved by seasons,
religion and the children of others.
They never married but picked raspberries,
dried herbs, and worshippingly sowed
primroses in the graveyard.

Far from Conway my grandmother
took pride in literacy, and planted a garden.
She submitted, and offered her daughters
no higher dream than she had dared.
She nursed caution at departure
from her own meek pleasures;
fearless too, in prejudice - but quiet.

Only my mother raged and wept,
tore the rope training her into service,
burst out with the brilliance of insanity
to test herself before she fell.

Stage Fright

I sit as still as a stone, still as a stump,
coaxing my mind blank. I'm stiff with will.
My brain's a swamp, a sweet sweaty wealth

waiting to be mined. The sump water simmers,
a stale pond. Small gilled fish flicker
just beneath the surface, their tiny scales

a glimmer in the muck. Well, is she winged?
Does she carry a stringed musical instrument?
Is she pure gold underneath? I have a lot

to learn. She appears, lugging that lyre
like a sacred harp. She's pale and blond
with a sharp boney face. She looks dead

144

serious and tired. She whispers: Take me
at my word, trust me,. I may be late, but
I wait for you, and just when you've given up

hope, I swear to you, I'll turn up like luck.

Steps

ADAM, perhaps,
thought of making a ladder when the fruit proved too high.
The high fruit prompted him to raise his eyes.
Eve said: Wait, Adam, the fruit will fall when it is ripe.
But Adam sat quietly dreaming of a ladder.

Gardens are not immune
to storm, to drowning. In time of flood a treehouse gives security.
Even the Queen perched above the ocean is pleased.
Blueblack she is, and beautiful.
The cool wind is the hand on the palm leaf.
If a fruit fall it makes an earthly thunder.
If Adam come, he climbs the steps with the grace of a king
and his plunder more precious than jewels.

Still. . . . .
the Ocean rolls in with a marvellous grin.
The fish leap/rising; down again—and under.
All the black waves, all the white sands
are the sun's, the moon's.
Adam said: Look, we are high,
where we have come is better than where we were,
here is our bed for moon and sun.

And the birds looked on.
And there was something said by the birds.
And Eve said: I will also say a song.

Up and down the steps go the children—
centuries and centuries of children.

145

The sky is the same - the moon is the same -
rains, winds: not a drop more or less of water
than on the first night Eve turned to Adam with a cry.

Up and down the steps go the children,
up and down the steps go friends and strangers
coming from across the rivers far from the origin
of the mothers, the fathers, the sisters and brothers.

Here are the steps of my own beginnings.
In this house I slept as a child.
In this house my mother wept, scolded, laughed, hated,
      and loved.
In this house I sat quietly looking to the horizon.

Qiuet, quiet now is the house.
All the fathers and brothers have gone away.
All the mothers and sisters have gone away.
The windows are where they were—
the steps are where they were—
I will go up again - and remember.

Stone

'Das Dasein ist rund'
— Gaston Bachelard

OGLALA DAKOTA

In the beginning everything was made round
except stone.

Sun, earth, moon are round
like shields; the sky
      a deep bowl.

Everything that breathes is round
like a plant's stem.

146

The circle stands for everything but stone:
the four winds travelling
at the world's edge,
for day and night when the moon
goes round the sky.

Therefore
we made our houses round,
our campsites circular,
and sat in circles when we ate.

I used to shut my ears when old men
passed the sweetgrass round
and spoke of stone;
it was the heart of those who ruined us.

We were deceived
by their sky-blue skins
and uniforms of indigo;
watching them in their tents and yards
all edged with stone
we wondered why they rode in lines
and laid down iron roads
on plains
that flowed with game and wind.

MAORI

Like wind far off
with great grave steps
came the rain.

Across the river
men with guns
slipped darkly on horseback
down the scree.

I called out to them
but the river drowned my voice.

I wanted you to tell me the darkness
was merely dark green,

147

our salvation the silver light
                    along the ridge,
that it was you we glimpsed
                    at the edge of the clearing
                    through the rain,
that your love would come to us unbidden,
the circle be closed again.

I wanted to hear that the darkness
                    was filled with snow-fed streams,
that our broken staves our fences
our plough lines our language
our songs our plantings
our selves
would soon be mended
by your words your promises
by a carved house
by the five voices
by the clover leaf, the diamonds, and the stars

Mihaia,

yes, and I hoped your voice
would recall for me,
my mother singing
                    in the rainbow room,
wild plums under windows
                    where we threw the stones,
women with lacebark kits
            bringing flowers and evergreens,
card players on a grey blanket
sheltering under a lean-to from the snow.

ACHAEA

The chorus began
in the noise of a threshing floor;
the navel of the earth
was a net of grain
flung round a stone.

A snake like a necklace
of onyx and emerald
drank at the air
then slipped through the ruins
at my feet.

By a cold spring
in a handhold in the hills
surrounded by cypresses,
the inarticulate syllables
of a wild girl.

At Epidauros
crushed laurel and sage
in a cupped hand

In the labyrinth
fat and limping citizens
dream their therapies

The scored bark of pines
bleeds resin
for wine

A mason's mallet echoing

Rain water collects
in a stone bowl.

The Aeroplane People

A sequence on the children of India

THE VILLAGES

You pass through my village, people behind glass. My wise cow
                                              ignores you.
See how he grazes on straw and paper in the concrete yard.
This water I carry for him.

This dust is our gold, is the earth my mother stoops to turn in
the field,
Is the dung my sister works into cakes, is the walls of my house.
In the city you will see my father.
He lives in a house with neither walls nor roof.
Tell him - my cow is so wise he will always come home at night.
One day, in plastic shoes I will travel myself and tell him.
When you have gone, aeroplane people, I and my cow, with these
roving animals will trample out your tracks.
Our dust you may take with you. You will leave nothing here.

JAIPUR

I stand with the other children and watch you, aeroplane people,
People who carry possessions.
There is tinsel on my saree, a child on my arm.
See how our fingers point at our empty palms.
When we are grown we shall guide you round the palace. You will
give us rupees.
Give us now bonbons, stylos, the slides out of your hair.
An ugly girl may be too poor to marry.
In the factory
The bright colours of our dreams are wraithed in enamel upon
gold.
Remember our empty palms, aeroplane people.
Remember the tinsel and the smile on the ugly face.

VARANASI

We are too poor to need anything.
We stand and look at you, aeroplane people, people in the coach,
Asking for nothing.
From the dust between our toes, from the straw of our houses,
We will spin you a golden thread,
From mulberry silk, weave you cloth of gold to throw around
your shoulders.
We will see you at dawn, with the tossed marigolds,
Bulbuls, temple bells, unbels, by the brown burning Ganges,
Where the sun sets light to the ghats.
Aeroplane people, go away from us as flames go, as dreams go.
Leave us, who are too poor to ask anything of you.

AGRA

We are the children of Agra
And we live, Mummy Sir, in distressing circumstances.
We shall be turned out of our house.
See, we have written it on our papers.
Our writing is neat and teacher is pleased.
Our laughter is as lapis lazuli honed on a turning stone
To be set in a momument that will never be built.
Where have you gone, Mummy Sir, aeroplane people,
People who go into shops?
Have you not heard us?
We are the children of Agra, with sweet children's voices.

DELHI

Kilted and trousered, we are the children of Delhi,
The delight of India.
For our education—
Today we have been on a train.
Today we have seen the chair Mrs. Ghandi sat in.
Today, oh, we have seen a monkey
And today we have see the aeroplane people, people who smile
                                                           at us.
Now it's the lesson, dull, full of hard words.
We shall remember you, aeroplane people,
Dance with you tomorrow at the Delhi Oberoi.
Our education completed, we too shall be aeroplane people,
Smiling at strangers in far golden lands.

DELHI AIRPORT

an unspoken dialogue

It is time for me to leave you, my beloved.
It is time for you to leave us, my beloved.

You will care tenderly for our children.
I will care tenderly for our children.

See that they grow upright in all gentleness.
I will see that they grow upright in all gentleness.

151

Is there any tenderness in the land to which I travel, my
                                                      chosen wife?
Is there any gentleness in the land to which you travel, my
                                                      chosen husband?
In my empty hands there is only love.
In my empty hands there is only loss.

It is time for me to leave you, my beloved.
My beloved, it is time and tears and hazards of the journey,
Time and tears. . . . .

The Canticle of the Skeleton

Blessed are the bones of the feet,
  they have rhythm and walk on the ground.

For heel to toe is a leap and an answer,
  every step is a dance up and down.

Blessed are the anklebones,
  they hold the hinges of uprightness and speed.

For they are the hammer, they are the anvil,
  they forge the wheel, they run on fire.

Blessed are the bones of the knees,
  they know the way of the Lord.

By bending and breaking they are made perfect
  until they have no need of words.

Blessed are the thighbones,
  they are the cradle of song.

Lyre and lullaby and story by the bed,
  girl and stranger, they are mother and death.

Blessed are the bones of the hip,
  they are a valley of honey and milk.

Pasture and meadow, blossom and seed,
 they are the winepress, they are the wine.

Blessed are the backbones,
 they take the heat of the day.

For the shoulderblade is what is left of a fledgling,
 its dip and swing are the image of flight.

Blessed are the bones of the breast,
 they weave the wicker cage of the soul.

For only the foolish think the spirit is weak,
 in time it breaks free and is gone.

Blessed are the shoulderbones,
 they bear the cross.

For they draw the spear, the bow, and the lance,
 they take the shock of the gun.

Blessed are the bones of the elbow,
 they are a jolt and crazy surprise.

For even when the muscles let go,
 they conduct the live wire.

Blessed are the wristbones,
 they pull strings.

Flower and lever, doorbell and window and phone,
 they say hello, so long, good-bye.

Blessed are the bones of the knuckles,
 they open up.

For they are raised on raps and hard knocks,
 they are the teeth of the fist.

Blessed are the fingerbones,
 they make waves.

Harp and guitar, cymbal and trumpet and drum,
 they scale the rainbow, they scatter light.

Blessed are the bones of the neck,
  they form the corridors of silence and speech.

Town and temple and tomb,
  they raise the gates, they set the altarstone.

Blessed are the jawbones,
  they break the ice.

For their words sprout like new grass
  from a spring without end.

Blessed are the bones inside the ear,
  they hear the truth.

They never stop listening,
  they are a bundle of nerves.

Blessed are the bones that shelter the eye,
  they are the quarry of sight.

Their veins are races of crystal,
  they are the light pipes of the mind.

Blessed are the skullbones,
  they are the mask, they are the theater of the soul.

For the stars walk in their sleep,
  and the flames radiate.

The City Revealed

A city, remember, wears its face at the centre;
From there its secret innards radiate. It exists
In non-Euclidean space, having turned itself inside-out.
Stand at Waterloo Bridge, or in Trafalgar Square;
You know you are seeing the cared-for externals,
The face you recognise: but to probe deeper

Into the city's nature, into what is hidden,
You must work behind the surface, into that
Receding interior, among the clustered innards
(Distasteful or disquieting), until at last
In Essex or the hills of Kent you reach its dark
Dissolving nucleus which an inversion of space
Has spread around. And from here, homesick
For coherence, for the look of the features you recognise,
You must retrace your steps towards the outside
And from Ludgate Hill or piccadilly Circus
See all again disposed in its proper place:
The innards decently contained within and you
Admiring the features, as is proper, from the outside.

The Cold Facts

from the collection
MULTIPLE ABRASIONS

In order to determine the distance to the
moon, we need only measure, in degrees of arc,
the distance the moon is apparently displaced,
against a fixed background of stars, when view-
ed from two different points on earth, each point
180° from the other.
if we consider the moon as the apex of a
right triangle, the base of which is the radius
of the earth, then, knowing the measure of this
radius and dividing in half the degrees of arc
described above thus yielding the angle opposite
the base we may by simple trigonometry ascertain
the length of the hypoteneuse i.e. the distance
to this celestial sphere   in order to deter-
mine the size of the moon we need only measure
the angle subtended by its image using a micro-
meter or such from any point on earth whatever
and knowing the distance calculated above we
may by simple trigonometry ascertain the size
of this celestial sphere

155

by similar methods we
might hope to find the distance to and size of
        the white violins
if only some direct some substantial observation
were made
as to their apparent location
and the image of the apparent size   that is
        the extent of the area they constitute together

to date we know only that they float in ocean waters
        #1 they have been sighted from
                pleasure boats
                these 'observations'   very brief
                white dots slipping over the horizon
                music lovers throwing themselves overboard
        #2 tidal effects
                can only be explained by the influence of
                the violin
                (viola and violoncello have been post-
                ulated but without
                                supporting data)
                tides constantly changing
                white violins remain at sea

and that they are white
        #1 absorbing the moon by night
        #2 rejecting the sun
        white light   is stronger   than   yellow

several hypotheses as to why they absorb and retain white
        #1 they are made of ice
        #1a they dislike passionato
        #2 it is part of their intrinsic nature

objection to #1a: they play the ocean
                        to rise and swell
                passionato is therefore
                either
                        in their own interests
                or more strongly
                        to use the words of hypothesis #2
                "it is part of their intrinsic nature"

Objection To 'objection to #1a': passionato
                           cannot account for
                           trough

OBJECTION TO "Objection To 'objection to #1a' ":
        trough can be thought of
        as an extreme of degree
        not a difference of kind
        i.e.
        *dis*passionato
        as opposed to
        a-passionato

the question of how many they are
        in number:
believed to be the source of tone signals received
        from the moon
spectral 'photographs' reveal there must be
        hundreds-if-not-thousands
        of these white instruments
when the spectrum shifts to blue the moon is moving
        closer
        in favor of music
        the clarity of the moon
           near the ocean
when the spectrum shifts to yellow to orange to red
        the moon is moving farther away
        repulsed
        the vagueness of the moon
           near the sun

important factors in this spectral analysis
        1) the frequency of the music
        2) how played
           crest or trough
        3) the wavelength

                  having determined the
size of and distance to the moon there can be
but one course of action if we want the facts
concerning these violins —
        #1 set up sensing devices at two different
points on the moon each point 180° from the

157

other   both devices must have   perfect pitch
and the same sensibilities as the moon (else a
conflict of interests during a blue shift or a
red shift)
      #2 activate the sensors to track the signals
coming from the oceans of earth
      #3 measure   in degrees of amplitude   the
distance these signals are displaced   against a
fixed background of music   Schubert   Brahms
for example   would be better than   say
Stockhausen
      #4 consider the white violins the apex of
musical accomplishment   the base of which is
common consensus
      #5 knowing the reliability of general opinion
 and dividing   in crest and trough   in node and
antinode   the amplitude described above   thus yield-
ing the eccentric degree of genius   opposite the
base   we may   by ample trigonometry   ascertain the
length of the hypoteneuse   the distance between
our sensory devices and the sources of all this
      #6 in order to determine the area they con-
stitute together   we need only activate one lunar
device to measure the rythm of the signals sub-
tended by the floating image   using a metronome
or such   and knowing the distance calculated above
we may, by amplified trigonometry, ascertain the
breadth of our ignorance

      now this plan can, admittedly, only take us
so far. However, we will be able to hear them quite
clearly, locate them, exactly, once we colonize the
moon.

      It has been suggested that perhaps black vio-
lins float on the oceans of the moon. Black dots
slipping over the horizon. Just another music lover
overboard.
      Mere speculation.

The Diary of the Delphic Oracle

1

My job
is to tell people
who have come to me for help
that they will win their lover,
war or treasure
the moment they quit hoping.
My job is to tell people
to give up.
I love my work.
Except when Cassandra comes to taunt us,
says the future takes no effort,
says the real work
is to tell the past.

2

Today I horrified Ulysses
in his business suit.
I told him he would have to choose
to love or trust Penelope.
He wanted both
and argued.
It was sad to watch his body,
all that helpless strength.
I told him
it required seven years' adjustment.
He said he didn't like to travel.

3

Penelope complains
she doesn't know
if she can love Ulysses
while he's gone to war.

I tell her
questions can be thrilling.
She says everything is ruined:
she has no power
for denying men.
I tell her surrender
is want with its claws in.
She says she has no life
beyond her suitors.
I tell her
it's related to the need to shower
before sex.
She says she hates
Ulysses' love for order.
I tell her
the worst things she imagines
will come true.

4

To Telemachus

As long as you're alive
you will miss your father.
You will seek his features
in the company of men.
As long as you're alive
you will be drawn to the broadshouldered
and the nearly tall.
You will know the thrill
of feeling helpless
among the large of hand.
As long as you're alive
the sea will cause you sadness
and the urge to look.

160

5

To Teiresias

I remember when you used to walk unaided,
when you could see trees in the distance
distinct from their mountains,
when your insight was frightening
and no one dared disbelieve you.
I remember when you used to be my competition;
for years I saw no one from Thebes.
I even remember your parents,
how you hated their mortality
and their dirty feet.
Now you're old and blind
and your reputation's as uncertain
as the boy who's supposed to walk you.
Don't give up.
It's true, the city
you have always loved
will perish.
The people that you love
will fall away,
and before the day is over
Oedipus will want to kill you.
But don't give up.
After everything has ended
you will come here,
the past burned from you like weight,
and you will join me,
the eternal, knowing vapor.

The Grey and the Green

> "Natural objects are *what we were*. They are what *we should again become*. We were nature just as they, and our culture, by means of reason and freedom, should lead us back to nature."
>
> *Schiller.*

I'm writing lazily upon
A day in late July, from Wales,
With nettles standing by the wall,
Grasses uncomfortably tall,
And in the grasses, snails.

With such abundance I shall need
No theme, the theme is all about me:
The evidence in stone and oak
Of rampant nature's only joke---
That she can do without me.

However riveting her glance,
I turn my back for half a year
And flowers are standing from the slates,
Spiders are spinning like the fates
And funguses appear:

Wet lips and frills upon the plaster
Like fairies kissing through the ceiling
Show how the rain induced the roof
To cease from standing so aloof
And to respond with feeling.

Rain! It's always up there, busy.
Sometimes it patters like a mouse
Or drums in boredom on the pane.
It stops, and starts, then stops again
And eavesdrops round the house.

It drifts in clouds against the mountain,
Swells the streams and starts to pour

In torrents down the slopes behind
The house and in the house, to find
Its way out through the door.

Sometimes it thunders on the skylights
As though being poured out by a jug.
This brief but mesmerising rain's
Succeeded by the helpless drain's
Protracted glug-glug-glug.

The gutters weep whole afternoons.
The contents of the sky, displayed
In sheets across the fields, aim at
The grass as if to beat it flat,
A drop for every blade.

Within our fenced and sheepless plot
The grasses work their grassy wills.
Rye and timothy and dock,
They cluster at the step and knock
Against the window sills.

Natural things are what they were
And what we should become again.
Once we were nature as they are,
And lug about beneath our star
The matter we were then.

So should our culture (said the Romantic
German in that sowing season
Of the soul's freedom) rightly take us
Back through our paradisal acres
Through liberty and reason.

You can be sure I feel the pull
Of all nostalgic mythic Edens,
But oh, how very hard it is
To see that arguments like his
Lend their design much credence.

For liberty on our sense never
Kept house with nature in the raw.
I think of Milton (as I scythe

163

The tangled clumps of green that writhe
In freedom at our door)

Whose message was that temperance
Requires the energy it curbs,
As syntax shaping sentences
Is happier not with simply "is"
But much more active verbs;

That civil order shows the fairer
When mastering the pulse of riot;
That good is known by evil, just
As love springs from the cease of lust,
From fretful chaos, quiet.

The rage of the homunculus
To nuzzle in the blinding yolk
Requires an absolute devotion
We must deny, and no emotion
Insists that we must choke.

So my firm mowing arm controls
A green and sprouting commonweal.
The populations of the field,
Clock and seed and fruitage, yield
To government of steel.

Down falls the crested hair grass, reed
Canary, oat; the barley's comb
And timothy's thick tail; the tender
Tree-palace of the bent; the slender
Fox-tail and the brome.

Where something like a nursery stood
Of lecherous grasses yet unborn,
See now their ravings quieten to
A neutered peace I can sit through,
A deckchair on a lawn.

Where on my knee a book can rest,
Where on the page my hand can think,
Where in my hand the Edding edds

Through which the mind in humour weds
Passionless thought and ink.

The mind, it may be said, and what
Is that? The mind is grass, alas!
It's all or nothing, that's the trouble
(I ponder, on that velvet stubble,
With cushion and with glass).

It's either everything we must
Become, or it's a giant con.
It's something we're amazed at, some
Impulsion---or it's like a bum,
Something to fall upon.

Who would not rather be a mindless
Grass? Locked in that quilted field,
No need to feel that it's of use,
Pollen and root and primal juice
In a green tube concealed.

With no pretence at calculation,
Hope or fear or memory,
Its head reveals its simple needs
In tapered symmetry of seeds
Tip-toeing to be free.

Our heads have long ago exchanged
The simple green for black and white.
Our good is lost, we do not need it.
Or if we think we do, we read it —
If someone else can write.

From noisy theatres of life
Our heads are full of long retreats
Where self-appointed NCOs
Exhort us daily in foul prose
From even fouler sheets.

Sunday mornings are devoted
To the required responses, civil
Arguments and qualifications;

To self-sufficient explanations
And other sorts of drivel.

The paragraphs of prescience,
The columns on calamity,
Are always just a little late
And, though so true, congratulate
Their authors with a fee.

And what is written may be thought,
Suffered or performed somewhere.
We're told it is, but then the telling
Becomes the product it is selling:
How can we ever care?

In solipsistic boogie-packs
Of cultural bandage we skate deaf
Down the high-street of necessity,
Protected from its shouting by,
For instance, Brahms in F.

Such music tries to tell us that
The air is yearning to contain
Whatever consonance of passion
Happens to be the current fashion
Of disembodied pain.

Culture creates élites of failure
And heroes of those tortured wrecks
Who at its prompting are most prompt
To issue chaste denials, swamped
By the hopelessness of sex.

The adolescent grass is not
Ashamed, is never seen to blush.
No secret hankering occurs,
Nor each *amitié amoureuse*
Turns to a helpless crush.

It does not calculate or risk.
Pleasure's unknown and so is force.
It does not crawl across the bed
And is too steadfast and well-bred
To complete divorce.

Nor does it regulate in verse
Complete disruptions of its soul.
No sublimation of *tendresse*
Promotes an urgency to bless
Another's vital role.

For one grass of a certain kind
Is not much different from another.
Its blind asexual reproduction
Requires no tea-time introduction
And never heard of mother.

It's not quite envy that we feel:
The sturdiness, the ignorance,
The generosity, the stillness,
Show love as an absorbing illness
That makes a choice of chance.

And in that paradox we live
As in the aura of a crime
That we regret but made us rich,
Too conscious of a truth for which
There's always or never time.

Living a good way up a mountain
Above the natural line of trees,
We nurture saplings, ache for torn
Or wounded cedar, oak or thorn
And mourn fatalities.

Trees are annual calendars
And their expressive flags have taught us
To greet the spring. They're little babels
For many birds, pencils and tables
To please our daughters' daughters.

The lifetime that they take to grow
Is rarely ours. We feel a bond
Like that with age: memorabilia
To be respected, grave, familiar,
A little feared or fond.

We note the fruiting of the rowan,
If it's the year for bullace or
For sloe, or how much higher stand
The valiant Blackheath walnut and
The Oxford sycamore.

But most regret in this last winter
The passing of an ancient ash
Which air, that changed location at
Unlikely speed, disturbed and flat-
tened with an unheard crash.

But now, although it leans upon
One hinge of bark, new leafage shoots
From stumps the guilty wind has healed.
It dipped its elbows in the field
And there established roots.

If only our unrooted lives
When felled could simply change direction
And all our tall assumptions both
Be trimmed and find amazing growth,
A perfect resurrection!

The tree has found a way of walking
Not as our childhood stories told us
Through sudden supernatural strength
But through first tumbling its full length
Then growing from its shoulders.

A saint might get to Bardsey by
A slow deliberate prostration.
And such a gradual pilgrimage
Would postulate at every stage
A halting in his station.

And we could take our time like this
Were life as long as it is wide,
With no regretful glances back
At all branchings of the track,
A lifetime for one stride.

I have a notion, though, that even
So we could not much rejoice
At what we'd done or where we'd got to:
What *is* requires to know what's *not*, to
Exercise its choice.

Perhaps we need alternatives,
Perhaps we need to make mistakes.
The will unfortunately thrives
On possibility: our lives
Must rise---or sink, like cakes.

And now the bees are sawing flowers,
As casual in the endeavour
As if the petals on each stem
Had fallen open just for them
And the sun would last for ever.

And other creatures in the grass
Move in their leggy purposes:
A caterpillar scurries hard
Across the warm particular yard
Of hillside that is his.

A beetle, tilted in the green,
Gropes with his antlers for a purchase,
And even from my chair I see
Its blackness inching to be free
In tiny wavering lurches.

Down there are even lesser beings
Who do not have the need to walk,
Nothing to make them climb or stretch,
Nothing to carry, nothing to fetch:
They simply hug a stalk.

You'd need a microscopic eye
To see them blind and massed and thronging.
Although their grassy life seems bleak
It is a vertical, unique
Achievement of belonging.

Few other sounds: the distant snigger
Of buzzards; the complaining tones
Of sheep; the crumpling of the small
Stream as it makes its shallow fall
Over the worn stones.

And always the sun arcing above
The fret that creeps below us still
Like a brave hand that quietly clears
The sky of its forgotten tears
And sends them down the hill.

It times itself across the mountains:
Tre'r Ceiri's nine o'clock, at three
The middle mountain, dusk the quarry.
It hangs upon the promontory
And sinks into the sea.

It's no surprise to find the sun
Intoxicating: we drink deep,
A summer's depth, a draught imbued
With every idle summer mood
Of love or wit or sleep.

Imperious season! It calls us up
In our unusual calm and fitness
Willingly to mount the stand
And take our future by the hand
In unreliable witness.

As though we just might go on living,
Our testimony never waver
And our condition be the same,
Always to have a right to claim
That judgement in our favour.

But summers come and summers go,
A flourish on the signature
Of the year's cheques, and we the claimant
Of punctual everlasting payment
Have no right to be sure.

A voice is calling down the field,
A trick of the light, or in the ear

The slightest shift, a distant saw,
A sudden rapping at the door,
Brings that familiar fear.

As harvest bends beneath the wind
Or trees are stirred and grasses bowed
When it disturbs the valley's surface
From the chilled wood to where the turf is
Darkened by a cloud.

Until the darkness that our lives
Will unavoidably arrange,
We have this pact to keep in peace
Our favoured landscape till time cease
To hesitate from change.

And Never is a world away
From Now, as Other is from Me.
The solipsist will never find
That time weighs heavy on his mind.
Self is eternity.

As on the mountain starry moss
Lies open to the sky unseen:
Proliferating radials are
A perfect mockery of star,
Pale on the darker green.

And yet those systems so like eyes
Are wholly inward, slow to change:
No observation, no reflection,
No intercourse and no connection,
Sightless, profuse and strange.

Is mind to be compared with these?
An accidental peal of bells?
Astronomy's congratulation?
Random organic integration,
A colony of cells?

You will not find the elusive mind
By cutting up a living brain,
As well might fronds of wire be seen

To sprout up from a grey machine
Or grasses rust in rain.

Our new computer in the eaves
Copes with the problems we have set it.
It finds square roots, defines an arc,
Plays asteroids or J.S. Bach
Or anything we let it.

Between the keyboard and the screen
Lies hidden electronic finery
That turns what either of you says
Into electric impulses.
Its simple code is binary.

It makes with anyone who chooses
Its Mephistopholean bargain
To help you to achieve your goal
Provided that you lose your soul
And use the proper jargon.

But I am not with those who fear
Its speed and rational procedure,
For as a model of the brain
It's much superior, it is plain,
To such things as Ouija.

The only problem is, the thing
Is motiveless, immortal, neuter.
You look for something like a mind
In vain, for all you'll ever find
Inside is a computer.

And what it does is limited
To what its program makes it do.
The power of the computer buff
Can only prove, alas, enough
To see his program through.

And that elusive element
Beyond determination still
Eludes. No god could tolerate

A being that he must create
In bonds, without free will.

A tool then, not a creature which
Is appetitive though obedient
Through recognition of its good:
It lacks that one misunderstood
Mysterious ingredient.

What do we call it? Nature? Life?
Where do we find it? Beyond the stammer
Of electronics freely move
Millions of nouns that seem to prove
An independent grammar.

Beyond the slavish rigmarole
Of subroutine and variable
The soft world's at its nightly ruses.
The tiniest midge still somehow chooses
To find itself in trouble.

When all the sun there is touches
The sea, and grey invests the green,
Eater and eaten flitter by,
A demonstration to defy
The passionless machine.

Horny and muffled moths whir through
The window, summoned by its glow,
And in the park of its display
Quizzing each Goto and array
Stroll stiffly to and fro.

The moon itself, the light they think
It is, is no less readable.
Its hieroglyphics are the history
Of an unfathomable mystery,
The grave celestial pull.

What wonder that the dandy moth,
Preening itself in its fur collar
And muttering in its whiskery muzzle,

Ignores the lesser luminous puzzle
Of waiting Inkey$?

So it might wait for ever if
No one could see its flashing cursor,
In a vast emptiness, unfree,
Deserted by humanity
(Or perhaps vice versa).

For if a desert is in question,
It's possible machines will make it.
The world, which has not lasted long
And may not, is going for a song
And no one wants to take it.

Should we bequeath it to the moth?
It needs some strange nocturnal creature
Like the gowned bat that haunts the house,
A crucified aërial mouse,
A tiny baleful preacher.

A world of bats and cold machines!
I do not find the thought endearing.
Programs survive though current fails,
Inscrutable as the bat's wails,
Voices unheard, unhearing.

The universe is full of noises
And rather fewer ears. The gift
Of sight is rare enough for stars
To die unseen. We can touch Mars
But galaxies go unsniffed.

It is our aim to use our senses
Rightly, senses of every sort.
Computers are a harnessed force,
No revolution; they endorse
Traditional ways of thought.

It's hard though, not to feel that when
I play a game of chess with one
It has a personality.

It gives a bleep to welcome me
Whenever I switch on.

Two pairs of OOs move up and down
As though, while pondering, it scanned
Visible possibilities.
God knows, though, what it really "sees".
Nothing that's not been planned.

Those tell-tale traits I find attractive
Mean all that its instructions mean.
Its program tells it what to do.
Nothing it does is really new
Or entirely unforeseen.

It doesn't joke. It plays five games
Straight off and doesn't mind five more.
It won't admit a move is clever
Or make illegal moves. It never
Offers me a draw.

It doesn't like a glass of something,
Ignores all flattery, loves to play
The French Defence and risks its neck
Through ignorance of discovered ckeck
More than a move away.

Losing the endgame makes it most
Like a person, least inert:
It gives up the defence, plays wild,
Moves distant pieces, like a child,
Hopeless, defeatist, hurt.

And such, perhaps, we really are
If mind is only an illusion,
A more or less determined process,
Part of itself, a true hypnosis,
A triumph of confusion.

Arraigned in our material being
The sentence of the court is binding:
Mind is the evidence we show

Of knowing that we do not know,
Of minding, and not minding.

It is the evidence and judgement, too:
Our mindfulness reminds us of it
At all those times when ignorance
Of what we call our loss, by chance,
Might turn it to our profit.

Fatal cognizance! As though
A frown in the flower means it fears
The absence of the bee---instead
Of some decision to be red
Until the bee apears.

Or yellow, plain, fantastical,
Long-lived or short, but never knowing
The pride of colour or the term
Of life, nothing beyond the firm
Root and grip of growing.

For flowers, mind is only touch.
Green is the colour that began it,
Green is the sign of the cell's toil,
A touch of sky, a touch of soil,
The ladder of the planet.

Green is the negative of the stars,
Green is the mirror of the sun,
Green is the cooling of earth's fire;
A height from which we have reached higher,
But the best thing we have done.

A daily hunger tells us we
Are planet, too. That is our root,
Ingesting green. Our meals should prove
We have a root at a remove,
A liberated root.

The body is not user-friendly
(Examples of it we have hugged
Show that its program, though involved,

Still has procedures to be solved,
Commands to be debugged).

Perhaps too liberated, then,
A simple hunger turned to greed?
Imperious inorganic lives
Inform us that mere being thrives
Without that cycled need.

A mountain is a mountain is
Itself, lasting, indifferent, proud.
The poet on his human throne
Has often wished that he were stone,
Or fluid, or a cloud.

Grasping the palpable, he feels
All that is vagrant in him lift
At the touch. A single fragile link
Offers an anchor he can sink
Into the friendless drift.

And now even the thought of these
Completed peaks, purpled above
Their green and still-grazed shoulders, brings
The shaping calm of well-loved things
Outside our human love.

Whose blessing is unspoken like
An institution's is to those
Who freely seek in its employment
Their chaste hopes and loyal enjoyment
So that it never goes

But stands for all time in the shape
Of what it is and has been, till
Its fond dismissal sets us free
From it, and life, and all that we
Might be and never will.

So in the shade of the three mountains
I sit from day to day and teach
The inward eye its signs: from ledge
And scree they run, from slope and hedge
Down to Will Parsal's beach.

Mushrooms put up in the fields
Where lofted thistles sail and spill.
Three horses come for sugar, late
Against the sun, and by the gate
The lane leads down the hill.

We are at peace here, where the grass
Extends however far we roam
And we can be, without having crossed
A road, tired out and almost lost
In a wood, but nearly home.

It is the world, and so it should be.
And it is ever so, once seen,
For the mind has caught it in its season
And there it is, and for no reason:
The grey among the green.

Lines from The Idylls of Sumeria

Sun-up

1 : Morning invocation to Our Lady

>Big-mouthed you are , swarthy , quick , sooty , lame ,
>   cast in the left eye , bearded in the morning - yet lovely
>   beyond loveliness we say you are !
>For you are ... you are the young woman , the old woman
>   the green girl , the old cow , the clown-goddess , the
>   lady of beer , the lady of bread , the barleyfield ,
>   the bedpost - bitter-sweet apple , mountain and
>   datestore !

The darling of the town you are , Inanna - the moon your
    mother , the sun your brother , what a family is yours !
    Amanamtagga the guilty one is your maid , and your
    cicisbeo Ada of the storms .
Oh your waist , Inanna , your slender waist .

2 : I have been the ibex

    I have been the ibex in the morning where the sun kisses
        the sweet , the drinkable water , where it drowses ...
    Have worn the astonished face of the water-ibex , have
        stared through the steam of the early sun's passion ,
        through the lifting of the water to the sun .
    Slowly the sun ... slowly the sun god Shamash raises his
        face from the stubble of reed , his cheeks burn from
        the stubble of the waking earth ... the god is up !
    Light flares off pools of sweet water - the irritated
        ibex backs and vanishes .
    It is dawn on the Lower Sea , and the snake-god Ningizzida ,
        too hot on his rock , slides to the water , saying as he
        passes , of the people of the shore ,
    " There go humans , feet in the water , heads in the sun ,
        date-palms who can walk " .

3 : Hi !

    An early riser on my two feet , fingers of sunlight probing
        the watery air ,
    I saw an angular shape down by the water's edge , horn of
        goat and hand of human .
    My breath took fright in my throat to see black horns
        against the sea horizon , white hands scooping the
        water .
    The shape parts , it is a goat abstemiously placing one
        foot in the sea ; and a human , rocking on heels ,
        who straightens to the upright , one fluid movement ,
        it takes your breath .
    I am going dawn-fishing with my darling for pearls , for
        snake-spit in the valve , we are to take the boat .
    And he is up before me . Hi !

4 : Girl's dawn song

My brother , tell me my brother , if the sun - no , listen
    to me , my brother -
If the sun were ever to leave his amusing lazy watery
    lover ,
If he were to leave alone the Lord of Eridu , were to forget
the Lord Enki , uncle of Inanna -
But suppose it were to happen , just suppose it were to
    happen -
And he lit on me , out of all Uruk he were to light on
    me ,
Should I have planets for children ? Would there be more
    than the five , because Shamash slept with me ?
The sun in the night ... think of it , my brother !

5 : The town-boy still in bed dreams of oystercatchers on the shore

Are the women salty there by the shore ?
Give me a taste of your tongue - don't wash , lady ,
    don't wash , swim and come to me .
Walk through the town slippery as a fish , leave moist
    footprints in the dust on the stair , to amaze my
    sisters and my brothers and my mother .
Step past the mats of my brothers on the roof here in the
    shadow of the temple , under the E-Anna .
Step to my place , shake , if you like , your hair so they
    wake - so they open , these my elder brothers , their
    fast-asleep eyes , and each on an elbow watch you into
    my arms !
Don't wash , woman of the shore , bring the scratches of
    the rocks on your feet , and a pearl in your mouth , and
    your hair salt from the sea .
Choose me , choose me !

The cool of the night

Lady on the town

She has climbed a step
To lean on stone still warm from the body of her brother .

She has cupped her chin in her hands ,
She sniffs the salt and sandlewood of skin ,
She is brooding , she is ready to make her move .
She has risen in the sky , turned the cheek of her evening
　　star ,
Has loosed the city for night , the horror of noon
　　forgotten .
She is the life of the city , and is alive tonight .
Dressed up !
She is in her diadem , soft white leather , and lapis-lazuli .
She is contemplating Uruk with a maker's satisfaction :
" look at it tonight !
" The outer wall , where the cornice runs , it shines with
　　the brilliance of copper !
" The inner wall , it has no equal , touch the threshold ,
　　it is ancient !
" Climb upon the wall of Uruk , walk along it I say ,
" Regard the foundation terrace and examine the buildings !
" Is it not burnt brick , and good ? "
Warm rain from the moon drips on the blue sails of the
　　felucca ,
Drips on the torsos of rowers .
" Shall I not have him tonight ?
" I have waited in the heat outside the gate of the city ,
" I have waited to kiss those sunburnt eyelids ,
" To put my hand against the hair of his neck .
" I shall wait in the cool of the town ,
" And perhaps not this time be refused . "

Fragments from The Jade Suit

　　Flat boat on the broad river. Reeds by the bank. A man
Standing on his oar
Walks the water and moves slowly on.
Millwheel dips into the sleep of day.
A glittering stroke from the stream expires in soil.

181

The wind wiles from the distant horsemen.
Wars come amid the sleep of ages
Like clouds lending speed to the moon.
The trees remain. Illusions do not rock them.
Men remain. The horrors are forgotten.
And still the same ills will rise too soon.

About the same time that Shih Huang Ti
Began that minor mimicry of Earth
In which his honoured body would be buried
When history struck his own life from it,
Princess Tou Wan and her husband Lou Sheng
Ordered immortality from magicians.
      Jade from Sinkiang province came in bales
Packed over horses across the western wastes.
Fashion it may have been. Who's to say?
Tablets were carved and garments made
From those divine stones bound with gold
In twelve fitting parts to cover the body.
      And they were buried in this armour
As Shih Huang Ti entombed his armies
For such protection even the Tao appeared without strength.

.

.

.

And thus,
As written notes of song are reached and thrust by voices into
                                    motion
So Lou Sheng's soul moves on the wake of Tou Wan's leaving
And drives from the dark lumen of the cave,
Through rock and felted soil to surface air
Upon his course of freedom and desire.
.

.

.

Prince Sheng's flight ends and penetrates the hill.
Darkness breaks. Another chasm looms.
Here is the Middle Kingdom seen from afar.
Rivers running, seas breaking by a shore,
Mountains for a cupped hand.
Centred there a great casket bourne on gold
Reflecting waterfalls and stars.

From an occultation of the light
A voice riches his seeing. One resolute and weary,

    "Courtesies are no more. This tomb's maze
    Confounds no spirits. Should have
    Shamanized the chamber, kept you out.
    Five hundred buried scholars reach out to snare me.
    Be you not one - tortures reach this far.
        Tell me of my son Fu-Su, creaking by the wall.
    I know of nothing I did not bring in.
    A wretched court this afterlife.

    Are you Duke Chou? No.
    He would not wait the centuries for me.
    Ah. Dragon mind tests without caring -
    Could sleep a thousand years and rise without concern.
        I saw the past as repose,
    And the future as commands.
        Once the human seeds arose. Each child-bloom
    Was tended for itself.
    Might overrun its breeding, find new seasons.
    Ah. But settled men have greater purpose.
    Time can make our whims.

.

.

.

Cast upon the moment of T'ung Jen
And through the living map of Huang Ti's kingdom,
Lou Sheng sees one great field for ploughing.
. . . The corporality of restraint he wears again

.

.

.

In unfamiliar robes and unfamiliar pressure
He moves on bare plateau with hoarfrost underfoot.

    Talents rise and are consumed everywhere.
Eternal thoughts renew themselves.
The nomad knows these things - the mobile ways
Of trust and command consume the old within the young.
Young women in old leather,
Old men within unlimned skin rumble into heaven.
Nothing to pause over. No part of life
Inedible.

Over a rise the caravan closes
On the clipped ridge of new China's wall.
    Come travellers. Come the dispossessed
From the shallow distance to the gatehouse.
Your exiled court, that looks in and looks out,
Bears tidings in and tidings out, the only
Courtesy of life.

Silk the least of reasons
For sailing the Dialectic
For the gatehouse and companionship.
    We humbly sit by fires on the well-rounded ground.
In those packs with dyes and spice and cloth
Lie mathematics and astronomy free from powers:
Humbled and glorified.
    Glance at the 'little gentlemen',
Books and exiled learning fill the space of our economy.

    Men are so alternate. They have their seasons.
The Heavens remain the same.
Walled land to wanderer is
Unalterable duty and unalterable coin.
We lie at different points in the flesh of life.
We go to where the nourishment is, to where
The Earth breathes.

Even the familiar has its unfamiliar time,
Has its own life from which we part
As we part our friends, our lovers.
    Now that is a rare thought, a foreign thought
Rising beyond the wall.

The Landscape Artist Returns To His Native Trees To Discover Vision And Writes To His Mother

(An Extract)

Too hot today to walk the mile into town.
Three girls go past, Muses? Fates? Mulherons dressed
for church, for late confession.
Mother I've only painted today not sinned;
16 gum trees in wads of blue, white and grey.
There are a lot of cows shading outback
coming in for water and see me, easel and chair.
I don't look ornate or difficult, I don't confess,
it's not theology. I want to discern the tips of
buds, the breaking forth of energy radiant and so
the sunburnt fact I am studying trees,
dumb as the ocean but then, the patience and love
the vows the dedication to find enough
desire to forget I'm no exception, no wonder,
my heart broken for nothing like suffering.
Suffering Romantic wiles, the True Image Female Art took
my eyes and showed them backdoor scenes,
just degrading tiny strokes of suffering tiny
oppresive insults, I have to study for Ideas
for Large Sight. Not that I can't splash off a picture
true to all standards; I don't feel etc.
Mother, we don't all have to live, some of us
tempt our minds to know the wretchedness of
discovering the morning empty, the gum trees
walking two by two off to the creek.
You say: "Isn't it fantastic to see God in the branches".
I say: "Angels singing like kids at a picnic",
red noses and watermelon seeds on shirts and blouses.
Paint local colour, local people local
numbness to any awe ever young love found in
the sandy turns of the riverbank between logs
and nettles and disbelief that bodies work.
Actually, there is communion, a boy can
tell his mind to the sun and stars and made
of the girl up the block a young woman;

185

first she ever heard talk straight
through the veil of heat, dust and dreams.
It all makes sense once it is sense
and takes on harness and bit. I've seen
horses rigged and drove a pair as a kid
too young for school . . .
But then Mother, you know my past!
I return to remember how, close
to the truth the full lie is banal and
fall in love to my toes that trees suffer,
yet not one of them is a moralist.
You might gain to see the leaves work the light
like slivers of glass, mirrors.
Our mutual friend died only last week, fell
in the street, split his head, they say overwork.
He'd talk to my wife and the kids like a grandfather.
He never thought me less than stupid, less
than useless, less than to him wasted.
"All that knowledge, all them smiles . . ."
(Was he my father? Beyond scandal, was he
something more to old widow you mother?)
And his eyes with rage, the old man choking,
frequently he looked almost drowned,
always he'd shake my hand shake my arm and
talk of how much nonsense my work is when
placed beside my kids, beside their mother:
"Vanities!" I don't love pigments, there are
200 colours at least and how many unspeakable greens,
how many blues, that which exists best in the world,
how many blues, the colour of all colours, the
bluest of all blues, how many blues? I die!
At night I love, I sleep, I wake in dark
looking slowly, the light now a grey blanket
and clear I die!
One painting, no painting, identity is
like the leaves, a sliver, a mirror, no more!
I don't care if that sounds flat.
I run to my kids and them kiss like boy, like girl,
like alive dying people like me.
There is no use in any of it, I kiss my son,
my daughter, my children sometimes kiss me, sometimes
we all dance together, wife, mother, father me,
girl, and boy, us, people, we know! We know. The trees

seem to enjoy the event, I never paint that, but
what I did paint was our mutural friend's dying:
A RAGE OF VINES, A RAGE OF LIES: REGRET.
I'll send a photo next week.
The farm looks its best for ten years.
"Was anything done, was anything ever done?" . . .
Some child in me has died.
I know it's your money lets me be here and do this.
I won't defend the finances of Art, I don't
believe anymore I make Art, nor am I an artist,
that's too sympathetic, too in line, too straight.
It's only a hobby my contemplation, my
efforts to desist from farming and paint.
I'm not at peace, it hardly need be said,
yet, my doubt goes away. Someone steals the paw-paws.

Welcome back from England, welcome home
from Europe, welcome Mother.
Sorry in all that time I never wrote.
The way it looks to begin is graceless,
abrupt, like how the bush grows
after fire, too lyric and painful
singular, a tree for hours.

The Lions

She lives in the archaic hills with lion
and sleeps with him in lion's lair.
She hears the hush of lions
gathering at the head of the valley,
till night rises and the wind gets up
and stars prickle in the dust.
She stalks the lion stalk as darkness thins,
her paw like his set on the leather path.
At full morning she roars the lion's roar
till trees stand like antlers on tall deer.
Mounted like him on a crag she scans the plain.
With her marigold eyes she singles out her prey.

She bounds to bring it down, she brings it to lion.
After he has gorged, she gorges too.
She slumps like him in the shadow of the thorns,
all afternoon, and licks the ten claws
on her forefeet, like him.
In the cool of the evening, she raises her head
like his, to hear earth whispering.
She sees day and night caress at the river.
Rocks comfort her as they do him.
She is aware of emptiness.
The moon rises, a dry white pebble.
She pulls lion's heavy paws about her,
she curls against his under-side
and the quilt of his fur.
She laps beside lion at the pool —
she duplicates eyes and mask and mane.
She rasps without thinking.
She treads the shallows and barges him
into deep water to splash and play.

Gone are the days when she dreamed of
riding into men's villages
and men bolting in terror.
Now every tree shadow belongs to her.

With the death of lion she rampages,
seeking whom she can devour.

The lady of the lake speaks

"Our house overlooked the valley.
I'm not sure my father watched when I conceived
(he was a great one of binoculars), and Ralph,
whom I was dating, darted in and didn't care.
It all happened down there, down under that water.

Late August it was, the blackberries tainted
my petticoat; some bracken to the left

188

nearly covered us (we did give dad a difficult
time); game birds pussyfooted along and a doe
passed with her fawn, where it is now all water.

We married and it was a son. He came in a gush
of water. At least a bucket of the stuff. He must
have swum the English Channel ten times over,
the doctor joked. I sobbed: the afterbirth caused
such pain, though the child dived out so eagerly.

Ralph, stricken by the cost, went into
economics and he figured it would be cheapest
if he bought rubbers now in bulk. So that
when Doris came, he was sure she couldn't
be his. He washed his hands of it, he shouted.

It could be true. There was this travelling
teenage boy once, who thumbed a lift. He looked
so sad, with acne all over; a pip really, his shy
hands fingering swellings and pits. I guess
I cured him for at least a week . . . he cried.

It's such a beautiful idea and yet
I'm not sure. Those old-fashioned rubbers crack
when stored too long. And Ralph was such a meany:
he used the same ones over and over, cleaning
them each time with soap and water.

And Doris, she stuck to him, funnily enough,
and he let her. We haven't seen much of her
since she moved to the city and married
that cab driver. But with Andreas, our son,
it was different: both of us were fond of him.

Oh, I still remember, still remember; my mind
is covered with sores—they feel like water
in the joints—remember. The cold of the scales
always make him pee when I weighed him. A real
geyser. No, like a bursting dam, so much water.

The first time he walked was down there,
in the valley. I think he was after some bird
he'd heard in the bracken or a sly moving

changeling. Later, as a toddler, he was so proud
of the paper boat he folded and set adrift.

'I saw your boat,' my father told him, showing
him his field-glasses. 'Where did it go?'
Andreas asked. 'Oh, I followed it the whole way.
it went from our little stream into a bigger one.
Then it braved a real river with heavy waves.

But it didn't capsize. No, even the rapids
couldn't get it. And at the very end, I could barely
see it, a little mermaid climbed on your boat.'
'Really?' 'Really, she steered it free from
the sandbanks and headed straight into the sea.'

He had his good sides, dad. He went down
that night and searched for the paper vessel
with his torch, so that his grandson wouldn't realise
it was just a story. He found it, dried it flat
and kept it in his wallet between his credit cards.

About that time these rumours started
about the dam, and then the plans were drawn,
we saw it in the papers. But Andreas and I
went down each day. Later on he played there
in that same spot, with friends or by himself.

It took years. The people lower down
Made lots of dough. They weren't selling
cheaply. Dad had only a barn and some sheds
just inside the designated area. Hard luck.
But he'd get enough to buy a new cooker.

They started pouring concrete. Dad watched it
going on, from that window, the closed one.
The dam was over halfway up before
the money came. Then Ralph crushed the old stove,
took the bits and threw them on the land.

The water rose and kept on rising. My father
started coughing, it sounded like gurgling,
as if he himself was filling up. When he died

190

our roof started leaking and in the morning
we found a lens of water on his coffin.

Andreas didn't cry much. But he got these dreams
in which he saw his grandad drifting downstream
in a coffin covered in headlines: RAIN TOMORROW.
Stopped by the dam, the lid opened and dad
rose up peering through his binoculars.

Other times he saw how the long green leaves
of the drowned bracken moved under water like
outspread tails of green hair, with slender
grey-eyed fish moving in-between. It made me
feel uneasy. I was glad when he went to college.

He started fishing in his holidays.
Not that he caught much, but one day he brought
a girl home he'd met on the waterfront.
She hired a motorboat and together
they sped across the lake. Or drifted.

Ralph got dad's glasses out. Trust him.
'Guess what they're doing,' he grinned at me.
I thought they all were on the pill, but she
was certainly a different type of girl:
within three months it looked like nine.

'Mum, she's carrying like you,' Andreas cried,
'look, what a tremendous swimming pool.'
She looked at him with her grey eyes. And as
she was too heavy, he went boating alone,
wind or no wind, till the boat capsized.

It stayed afloat, upside down,
but no trace of him. They searched for days.
One night the girl was standing outside,
her lank hair lolling in the wind. She saw
me staring. So I opened the window.

'It must be because I was crying,' I explained,
'but your hair suddenly looked so green.'
That night she stole Ralph's car and went.

Later—after that funeral without a body—
it was spotted at the Greyhound station.

That was the last we saw of her. We have
no idea if she kept the child, that changeling.
Yesterday I found two rings from our old stove
(the flat ones off the top) like Ralph and I—
never linked, and now bound by rust.

Oh yes," she pointed, "Ralph nailed
those shutters and covered them in board.
But there is still this glint, you must
have noticed it, this glint of water."
She stood up to make coffee.

Spilled water gurgled in the sink.

*The New Internal Combustion Barge**

One brilliant summer day
Of white clouds, bees and hay
And flag and festival,
A barge without a horse,
Impelled by its own force,
Was launched on our canal.

Our school turned out to see
This curiosity,
This pretty painted barge
That chugged along the stream
Propelled by puffs of steam,
One engineer in charge.

The boat was laden down
With gentry from the town;
The Mayor had brought his train
Of aldermen in hats

Like chimney-pots, white spats.
Each sported a gold chain.

The wives, in purple silk,
Complexions pale as milk,
Held parasols and fans
Protecting ostrich plumes
From spots of dirt, and fumes,
And stains from spilt oil-cans.

A three-piece silver band
Played from a small grand-stand
Tucked in behind the hatch.
The Chairman of the Board
(With blue cockade and sword)
(Knighted by last despatch)

Poured waterfalls of wine,
Invited all to dine
On drumsticks and ice-cream.
With napkins at their lips
The wives took gentle sips
Of champagne, in a dream.

We ran by the canal,
We cheered the unnatural,
Miraculous, display;
The boat, without a horse
Or sail, setting its course
Along our waterway.

The bandsmen played away.
Before the boat there lay
A large hill, dead ahead.
Into a pitch-black tunnel
That barely cleared the funnel
The puffing boat soon sped.

Our path stopped suddenly,
And all that we could see
Was the red brick archway.
Dark water softly lapped

Its sides, dank leaves were trapped.
The place smelt of decay.

We climbed the sunlit hill,
Slid down with speed, until
We reached the distant side.
Alder and willow clung
Over the slope, and hung
Where the canal ran wide.

We heard the little boat
Chugging its cheerful note.
The prow shot into light.
The late sun blazed with gold
On craft and paint, the bold
Brass fittings dazed our sight.

The three-piece silver band
Sent sparkles to the land,
Fob watches gleamed and spun.
The Lord Mayor's heavy chain
Had each link gilt again
To flash a separate sun.

The dazzling boat came on,
The halo round it shone,
And no-one moved or stirred.
We heard the engine's beat
Thickened by grease and heat,
But nothing else was heard.

We all fell silent too,
Stunned by the brilliant crew.
We could have touched each one.
The Lord Mayor, his brave train,
Aldermen, wives, captain,
Slid past us, and were gone.

But we had seen their stare,
Their eyes protruding glare,
As fixed as pebble glass;
Their faces, deep wine-red.
Each one of them was dead.
We'd watched a coffin pass.

Straight as a die, the boat
Swept on, with all afloat
Sitting there, bolt upright,
A set of wooden dolls,
Black hats, stiff parasols,
Lacquered with yellow light.

Inquest and coroner
And newspaper concur:
The tunnel had no air.
The boat had burnt it all.
Progress was our downfall,
Our pride was our despair.

*This poem is based on an old story.

The Pond

I

The Old Scientist and the Pond

I have waded in deep as an old man can
who is a worshipper of ponds and stars
because both are the holes into which
the dead things fall to be born again.
—A numb cold seeps in my toes, spills
past the warped leather tongue, bringing
a dozen ostracods and a bosminae school
to feed on the rich wool soup of my socks.
I have made myself one with this world
where the worn-out part of me belongs;
both the occupants I see now, and those that come
when its mud is swirled in a round glass jar.
I know about ponds, how they choke on the corpse
of success, how this one soon will be a

195

swamp, so thick that the long-toed dotterel
stamps on top. Now the shoals swarm under its surface,
the two-way light-filtering mirror that keeps
the saprophytes and stars apart; and I see
the pool on this leaden day as what it is—a cold
furnace, where forms are dissolved and made.

II

As a Child

Denied pets, I was king of millions: the Spring
tadpole shoals, water-boatman patrols,
fairy-shrimp flocks and murderous beetle gangs.
Water-fleas, the living sign of myriad,
pulsed in clouds like shy galactic swarms
lost in their own plurality. Misting
the red decaying leaves, diatom nebulae
linked spiral arms. The bumbling ostracods
spread randomly like asteroids. Fast-pulsing
cyclops fed mayfly larvae, damsel-nymphs,
and water-striders whose snow-shoe'd feet
pushed down six sun-reflecting dimples
in the pond's hard top—I knew the dogpaw
pattern of their shadows on a smooth mud floor
from which the bubbled gnats burst up to plop aloft
on wings that did not fail. Whole hordes and races
passed uncounted in this world I guarded,
not knowing its true manager, the seasons

Escaping family quarrels
I'd come each month to find the tribes
of favourite subjects vanished, others instead
gambolling for my attention. After long search
the last fairy-shrimp was found in weeds
of a later month. The dance of bosminae
feasting on glassy rod-bacilli
was part of the autumn spiral of decay
that led to a finger-numbing clarity
when giant winter daphnia crowded in the depths
bouncing slowly in light of a slant sun,
till sharper shafts slipped through
to cloud the pond with a Spring ferment, brewing
old leaves to humus and sweet water.

The day the brick-trucks came
I was twelve, and saw the universe destroyed.

III

The Old Man Considers the Surface

Strange that the dark soup of life prefers
to ripple back an abstract sky, bending
light from before the Iron-Age wars.
You can see Alpha Crucis in a pool
sooner than what lives one foot under.

The striders dance on their siamese twins.
How they ride these wavelets my knees make!
I remember now that the surface
of water is busy as roads; with
rain-ripples, stick-wakes, leaf-tremors,
bird-skim and slow back-eddies . . .

I stare in this mirror that inverts the world.
The Ram spins as a whirligig
razors the surface, that weeping-glass
where the moon counts her witnesses
on cloudless nights. A signal dish
for lonely stars? or a hit-man's
polished sunglasses? I know that it hides
what enters, offers back a diminished world,
is a frontier only the kingfisher's beak
and hawk's claws penetrate.

Soon, for a moment, I'll fracture that mirror
and sink through the constellations.

IV

The Black Hole

The crab's many legs make me feel a cripple.
I cannot trust one who will walk, snatch, scrape
eat, kill at once.

My thighs take the chill. Bloat meat
in the water embarrasses some,

197

but the pond can digest, is a sort of stomach
ceaselessly putting forth lives. I watch
how the crab sets two pair of legs to graze
the rich fuzz from a red oak-leaf,
plumping eggs for her coming Spring. Her
twice-twinned antennae twitch, sweeping the world
above, below, in a lifetime's habit of distrust
with no especial suspects. She forgets, I know,
which assassins ate her hatch-mates, though
the smaller ones crunch nicely now. Overhead
the bewhiskered mindless scullers drift
kicking food into their mouths, their fetus eyes
bulge with unfocused light: nervous crustacea
whose life is one frightened meal, alert,
with no preserved retreat.

The reed-warbler flutters down,
to take a struggling mouthful from the top.
The crab sidles off, shadow-wary, tensed.
Now she halts, irresolute on her oak-leaf stage,
mincing a meticulous, paranoid, octopod dance . . .

The spirogyra algae streams like green nymphs' hair,
its fruits pure silver spheres of air . . .

. . . How long was I gone in that other world
where the pond's black hole inverts?
Those roots intertwined, this ruddish ooze,
did I make or dream? The crab in another place
pulls apart a thin gray worm. The warbler
dips and flies.

                       Now I stoop
and a ripple disturbs the constellations.
Their former image waves through a red-leaf shift,
preparing my entry. The laws of stars
run riot round an old man's knees
and the crab comes now
sideways and hopeful, like a tobacco cadger.

The Red Train

I

The station's esplanade was thronged with faces
Like yellow pages full of hidden warning.
I had awoken to another world this morning.
Now men and women carrying suitcases
Brushed past me, their bright eyes grown wide with terror,
All victims of a Governmental error, —

II

Or something—I'm not quite sure what it was.
I stood before the barrier with my ticket,
Though no one was there to punch it at the wicket,
So I passed through, half dreaming of long grass
And the scent of trees in a parkland waving broad
Over hollows seen with love on old greensward.

III

A train sighed at the platform: driver and guard
Stood back to back, not watching anything.
An old man played with keys upon a ring,
A child jigged his bucket very hard.
I climbed into a carriage mottled green—
A vicar and two sailors sat therein.

IV

The reverend doctor wore a trilby hat
Pulled down over one eye like Al Capone's.
Through his translucent knuckles the sharp bones
Stood up in peaks. His raincoat smelt of cat.
"Have you boys been on leave?" he muttered, puffing
At a pipe overfilled with straggled stuffing.

V

"That's right, some leave!" one sailor said, whose gaze
Stared past his own reflection at a world

Of frozen chaos.—Mothers with arms furled
Sat on suitcases in the steam's hung haze,
(Pre-diesel the trains), faces drilled masks,
Pressed to coats, newspapers, baskets, thermos flasks.

VI

I looked for understanding from these men
Who sat about me in the mottled carriage.
The vicar talked of casual sex and marriage:
"I know you lads feel the need of it, but then
"We all do"—leaning forward from the hips,
Stroking his pipe-stem with corrosive lips.

VII

They talked together for what seemed an hour,
These men, and joked equivocally, without mirth,
At the propulsion of their setting forth
This day. The train moved. Suddenly a shower
Scraped at the window with provocative rain;
But I did not think I would return again

VIII

As on we trundled into a landscape
Of low-flung grasses sometimes sparsely bouldered.
On the horizon empty bungalows mouldered
Under the damp, their window-sockets agape.
The vicar's small eyes nervously perched upon
My face, then wavered away, to catch in the sun

IX

Which watered weakly from a cloud and scattered
In rivers forked upon the window-pane—
In diamond rivers of the wayward rain.
It was as if nothing had ever mattered.
Both sailors chewed indifferently, their eyes
No longer able to evince surprise.

X

Suddenly Nausea rose to my lips and spat
Out her witch's gasses in a stream
Of fear. Was I breaking in a dream?
"Where are we going?" were the words I shaped: whereat
The vicar's face froze; one sailor turned and said:
"Breakdown!" My heart hung heavily with dread.

XI

"Yuh, Breakdown,"—so, his chewing friend. The land
Loped past the window like a hurricane.
Perhaps, I thought, I am not really sane,
Nor have been ever. I did not understand,
But moved without into the corridor,
And, heaving cutting breaths, stared at the floor.

XII

I then moved toward the toilet in a spin,
My shoulder brushing the windowed doors of other
Grave compartments wherein sat a mother
With baby ensconced on her tweedy lap, a thin
Man dragging a whisky flask for relief,
His Paleolithic face a mask of grief,

XIII

And the girls, Denise and Evangelina, whose names
I knew somehow without having met them before.
Their skirts were hitched above their knees: the floor
Was strewn with remnants of their idle games—
Scrawled-on photos torn from magazines
Of a group of youths protruberant in tight jeans.

XIV

And then a child's voice, like a wavering bell,
Silvered the molecular air: "Soon be there?—
"At Breakdown Harbour Hospital Station where
"We're going, Daddy?"—"Yes, dear. Now, keep still,"
The father's voice returned. Round a bend in the meadows
Breakdown Junction veered, a tumble of shadows.

XV

No lock was on the toilet door, so I pushed
Against it with my back as nervously I
Emitted: beyond the window sat the sky
Across which presently a chimney brushed
Breathing asthmatic steam. The train squeaked near
The junction before I finished my function of fear.

XVI

I returned to the carriage like a hobgoblin blown in the wind.
One sailor wrested a kitbag from the door.
His companion peeled a thin packet and crammed yet more
Chewing-gum into his cheeks. Perhaps I had sinned,
And this was my punishment, but justice, whether divine
Or no, seemed unreal, not so much malign,

XVII

As absent, an illusory concept at most.
The sky was bound with a rope of cloud. We assembled
On a cold strip of platform and, mute there, resembled
(Faced, as we were, in all directions) the host
By Dante seen lodged and bowed on a narrow ledge,
Who could not, till a life time ended, budge;

XVIII

The Indolent stranded on a terrace of Trial
And Pardon. We were nudged into a queue
By officials with chattering cheeks, and two by two
Moved forward, dragging together in double file
Towards one who wore upon a cerise band
About his sleeve the words 'Red Cross Command'.

XIX

And then our train moved on with a wrench and a sigh
Leaving us suddenly gaping at the view
Of another train which stood at Number Two
Platform across from ours. A single cry
Drilled, for a moment, ice through the paralysed air,
But no one knew who cried, nor did he care.

XX

This other train was red as a pillar-box.
Upon its side the paint streaked like spilt blood.
I stood as though cold-chiselled out of wood.
About me, coughs tuned the air like the ticks of clocks.
Across two coaches' flanks, seen through the gloom,
Was written in hooligan letters: This is your Tomb!

XXI

No one about me seemed surprised, just nervous.
The vicar and his sailor-friends down the queue
Blew their hot breaths into the cold air: few,
If any, wanted to create a fuss;
All seemed insensate, threads in a machine
Who could not be what they had never been.

XXII

"Name, please," a quick voice said. I turned, and there
Before me he who wore the cerise band
About his sleeve was standing: in his hand
A square of paper pinned to a harboard square
On which our names were written. I now stood
At the sad queue's head, wondering if food

XXIII

Would ease my balanced stomach's trepidation.
The official took my name. "You will reside
"Tonight in Number Five," he said: "Inside
"That glass door there; it's alright at the back of the
                                                    station.
"You're sharing with three others, two of 'em Josies,
"— So *who* will be a thorn between two roses?"

XXIV

This inappropriate banter had me worried.
— The strangemess of it all! The dire air's hover
Scarce-breathing, with excitement, like a lover
Omnipresent and active! — So I hurried
Forth into the building on my right,
Where all was saddened by electric light

XXV

Dull and level, slack, and brimming over
Hardboard partitions flanking a corridor
Thick-smelling of disinfectant. The scoured floor
Lay blankly out before me: a sagging cover
Of canvas dampening hung above my head,
And bulged upon me as though full of lead.

XXVI

I found the room quite quickly. The frail door
Half-open, shuddered faintly, and within —
Four beds, with pillows humped upon them, clean
And white, stood stark upon a boarded floor.
Through the silence pinprick voices came,
Hovered and went, like moths about a flame.

XXVII

I threw my single suitcase on a bed.
It sat, pathetic. One clip had shot open.
I had no urge to move. I stood, a burden.
Heavily and slanting hung my head.
I had no urge to move. The silence pounded
About me with a blood-beat that resounded.

XXVIII

I stood, a burden, in this pulsing square.
Behind the room's one window a hard sky
Glowed out in silver, then commenced to die
Beneath a ridge of cobbled cloud. Despair
Comes into a more certain state of mind,
I thought, than that engendered by this blind

XXIX

And badgered groping. After all, it is
Finality, despair, wherein you drink
Only the tired dusk, nor can you think
Of other draughts as possibilities.
But I — pushed, desparate, against a square
Of wooden light — was not yet in despair;

Aggravation fidgeted my mind.
My own imagined laughter shook my breath
And guttered to a halt, as if swift death
Had lopped it short; an echoing behind
The silence after laughter was my own
Imagined voice vociferating alone,

But far away the ragged conversation
It held with its own shadow. I was peeved,
Uneasily peeved, that's all, nor yet believed
A fatal wingspan spread above the station
And all its inmates, like me honeycombed,
Each in his own square place, as though entombed.

Then through the door in burst a Bombadier
Of indeterminate middle age: his face
Was nicked with lines inscribing a grimace
Whimsical and tautened, without fear.
His eyes were those of birds that peek and prong,
Yet do not let encroachment halt their song;

He chatted merrily of this and that.
"Best billet I've had in ages this is, mate.
"I've heard the grub's quite good, at any rate,
"Though it's not a Naafi, is it? Wonder what
"You'll do when them two birds come in here. — Who's
"The lucky lad, then? — Hope they've got some booze

"Here in this place. Not like a Naafi, though,
"Is it? Been in the forces, have you?" "Yes",
I said: "Not very like an Officers' Mess
"Old boy, I bet, eh, what? — this place, you know?"
He chirupped — slit voice silting through his teeth
In mockery upon unhealthy breath.

XXXV

"I wouldn't know," I said, the tiredness rising
Within me like Lethe filling up a well
Of aching stone. "No? - It's hard to tell
"Who's Officers these days. It's not surprising
"We're in this mess now, is it? Bloody Hell!" he
Said. "What mess?" I cried, "Please, can you *tell* me — ?"

XXXVI

His face locked still, a mask of frozen mirth
Compact, as if to say: Well, don't you know?
No, I *don't* know, I shuddered through and through, —
My lips a-judder, my body Adam-earth
New-stamped by God, new closeted in sin,
New-tempered for a fight I could not win . . .!

XXXVII

When through the fragile door in came the girls
Denise and Evangelina. Smooth as husk
Their skins; like stripped birches in the dusk
Glimmering, their whiteness: auburn whirls
Of hair above each tiny visible ear
Were patted into place with frisky care

XXXVIII

As they perused the room with leonine eyes.
"Beds comfy, darling?" Denise said to me.
"Evangelina, look, we've company."
Evangelina did not theorise
Upon this observation, but instead
Threw herself down upon the nearest bed.

XXXIX

The tight springs danced beneath her body's thrust.
"So, who is going to be lucky?" the Bombadier
Said, smacking my arm, that chronic leer
Craning about his mouth. "Lovely, just
"Lovely," he murmured, eyeing both the girls
Whose coats sheathed their bodies like a tulip's furls

XL

Shielding the tender clitoris beneath
Closed but intact with promise. Cheerily,
My mirth like a dead fang, I turned to say,
"Well, you are lucky too" — and through his teeth
Informally lodged like grit, he breathed these words:
"I want Newcastle Brown. I've done with birds."

XLI

"What's going on here? Can you tell me, please?"
"I don't know, mate. I've heard that *they* have gone.
"Apart from that, who knows what's going on?
"It's up to *them* to tell *us*. Trouble is
"They never know, theirselves. But I'm afraid
"The train to Portling-Hoo has been delayed."

XLII

"But *who* have gone? Whom are you speaking of?"
The Bombadier merely released his belt,
Then clicked it fast again as though he felt
His stomach thinning underneath the rough
Time-chewed cloth of his battle-tunic. Then,
Without a word he went — and I, again,

XLIII

Fixed my eyes upon the window-square
Through which, between dark threads, the moonlight shone
Yawning like an avenue of bone
Between the lamps which blew but here and there
In a most haunted district of cold Heaven.
Night had fallen. It was half-past seven.

XLIV

Like Evangelina, now Denise
Stretched on a bed, and stared and stared at me
From under prone lids as, by staring, she
Would draw me on between her parted knees
Into a perfect vessel just careened —
For she upon her side towards me leaned

XLV

With coat flung open — winking dress beneath —
Awaiting hands to scour with delight
An hulk of promise in the fallen night.
Her tongue swelled to erection, and her teeth
Carefully tested the bud's pliancy,
As all the while her eyes eat into me.

XLVI

"Shall we take it in turns with him?" she said.
Confusion, like a briar, pulled my blood.
"Excuse me for a moment, if you would,"
Ironically I replied — and then, instead
Of levelling, concupiscent, left the room —
That half-shut, breathing, fiery honeycombe

XLVII

And took the passage blindly to a spot
Whence it levered off into a large
Hall the colour of netted camouflage
— Khaki and green wallpaper flecked with rot
Squared, staring at me. People stood
Annexed to a bar, awaiting food.

XLVIII

I watched them from the doorway. Others sat
About small tables, looking any way
But at each other. One who bore a tray,
Her stiff hair henna'd under a pinned hat,
Moved like a zombie haltingly between them
With disregard, as though she had not seen them.

XLIX

This smelling place was like a mausoleum
Housing just ghosts. I looked about to see
If any there showed signs of sympathy
With my intelligent confusion. Some
Attached to my eyes their eyes for a space,
Then dropped their eyes again, each shadowed face

L

Alone within a mass of human faces.
Like sculptures in a ritualistic round
They sat or moved or gently turned, the browned
Walls, cave-like, holding them to their places
Of uncomfortable rest, these passengers
Between two worlds, and each world thronged with fears.

LI

Some faces were familiar, but drained
Of the hard glow industriousness sets keen-
edged about such features as are seen
Flatly surprised in a flash, who, brusquely strained,
And framed by borders of newsprint, smile out
Upon a million readers quiet with doubt.

LII

But he who caught my attention most was one
Amid the postured ghosts, who, lean and tall
Above all others gathered in this hall,
Seemed a student, or perhaps a don,
With striped scarf thrown in wreaths about his neck
And falling in crossed tails down his back,

LIII

Loose-fitting jacket scarcely reaching over
The wizened posterior of his trousers;
His shoes were of the sort once known as 'mousers',
(Or 'brothel creepers', if you would prefer) —
And his face, ravaged with smiles, was beaconing gently
In all directions. Him I surveyed intently,

LIV

For he had knowledge I had not of whatever
It was made faces into masks this day —
Masks barely proofed against all memory
Of their own laughter running through a never
never land that is life in the sane and quiet
Garden free from echoes of ignorant riot.

209

LV

As I approached him he nodded and muttered closely
Something in French, but with a Churchillian accent.
I asked him if he could tell me what was meant
By all the day's proceedings. He obtusely
Remarked, my hairline rivetting his stare:
"The General and his good lady are gone from here. —

LVI

"But," he added, "on the whole it's quite
"Jolly." I turned, and through the door there came
An official whom I saw to be the same
As he who stood before me when daylight
Darkened over the red train, and whose arm
Had stitched to it insignia of alarm,

LVII

The words 'Red Cross Command'. "Please, can you give me
"Any information?" I enquired.
His mottled eyes were bland, opaque, and tired.
"No, sir, I'm sorry. Now if you'll forgive me,
"I'm very busy. Not that way!" he cracked out
To a figure who bucked and swivelled at his shout,

LVIII

One with a hat too large for him, whose eyes,
Paining under pebble-dense lenses, peeked
Into a stoniness fretted with faces beaked
And pincering . . . (I stood behind those eyes
For a second of shock and felt at once to be
In sorrow the quintessential refugee) . . .

LIX

This figure — no quilty Ahasuerus,
But God broken in Man again and again,
The eternal refugee of now and then,
O merely a Man Son of Woman, no more, no less —
Moved from a door admitting to nowhere
And casually into silence mouthed a prayer,

LX

Then stood, an image from old newsreels, still
Like all the others, delving emptiness —
An ancient figure in mortician's dress.
I joined the queue for food. At the far till
A woman counted change into the hand
Of a man who counted with her as though stunned.

LXI

I tried to summon memories of glee
— Of Harry Secombe, S.J. Perelman,
Groucho Marx, and all the broker's men
Whose laughter across dark hollows tickled me
And split gloom into dancing light that made
Sanity plus, and bigotry afraid.

LXII

But laughter was — as in a mirror — dumb;
The look of it I saw, but did not know
The feeling: ribs blown out, body a-glow,
Ease stretching over limbs. My limbs were numb.
By all means let us jape and ridicule
Futility out, but the square hall as here still

LXIII

And all the people frozen in a queue,
And the vicar alone in a corner, and the don
With ashen head grinning at everyone,
And ghosts pight in circles of silence. True
Humour in my mind was but a paper
Touched by a tight'ning fire that made it caper

LXIV

Prior to obliteration. Minutes passed.
No one spoke: and she who at the till
Had counted change before was counting still
Into the same man's hand. By panic harassed,
I left the queue and blundered through a pair
Of glass doors swinging into empty air.

LXV

I was in a passage barely lit from the door
And from two windows situated down
The semi-dark through which blue moonlight shone
And fell in slithered pools upon the floor.
The air was cold like a tomb's yawn: and fidgeting
I heard of paper blown or mice scratching.

LXVI

My shins were cut on lips of boxes. Around
I turned, around and again around to face
Always the moonlight threading through smeared glass.
I fumbled into emptiness, and found
Myself once more behind glass doors in the hall
Where still stood a stalagmite queue of ghosts in thrall,

LXVII

The woman counting change into the hand
Of a man who counted with her: faces waxed.
Never before had sanity been taxed
By such engraving shadows as were found
Here in this island of soiled light. The dream
Persisted — and was reality, not dream.

LXVIII

I must find the girls, I thought, and spun and sped
Through another door opening on emptiness
And reached another passage, hoping this
Would lead me to room five, my sullen bed,
And the girls undressing like flowers struggling from leaves
And bobbing naked and joyful, though silence grieves.

LXIX

Silence watching from discarded thrones,
Old thrones of mythological gold that moulder-
not in the neither heat nor cold of older
Heavens silent as a cask of bones;
A silence not of judgement but of thought,
Of thought that wonders till all Time be out.

LXX

I circuited many passageways, the walls
Turning upon me as I ran, and muttered
Happily the words Denise had uttered,
'Shall we take it in turns with him?'. The calls
Of siren-voices led me in a round
To always the same door at each dead end,

LXXI

A door marked Number Eight; attached thereto,
Beneath the number, was a purple star —
A blob of blood soaked deep into the door
It looked: no matter how I ran to view
The ends of other passgeways, always
I came to Number Eight from out the maze.

LXXII

Upon the third time staring at this door
A voice behind me pricked my head around.
Was it a man or woman there I found
Staring at me from damp caves before
These mouths of many passages? The head
Of this creature was yellow as though dead,

LXXIII

The bones looked haunted in the tired face.
It said: "You can't go in there. Look, the star.
"That was the General's room." "Which General? Where
"Is Number Five?" I said, "do you know, please?"
"Oh, yes" it sighed, this Angel at the crossroads,
This yellow hermaphrodite from dark abodes;

LXXIV

"Turn right, turn left. Turn left, then right again.
"And take this passage here." I thanked my guide
And trod the dark, lust blooming in my seed,
My head pressed to the dark as though in pain
And seeking salve upon the night, to arrive,
Quite happily and drugged, at Number Five.

LXXV

Both girls were there as when I'd left the room.
Denise, her hair a helmet, sat upright
Cocooned by bedclothes in the level light
And, when she saw me, squealed and slithered from
The pillow her bare back rested on; one knee
Up — as her eyes intruded roguishly

LXXVI

Into the firmness under my stretched fly.
Her cheeks bloomed out and sank as she sucked a sweet —
A massive humbug revolving, pointed and neat
As a tulip-bud or a wasp's end or an eye,
Peppermint-tingling, striped like bombazine,
Which pulsed her cheeks from shadow into sheen.

LXXVII

Evangelina stood (having discarded
Her outer clothes) in a ragged leaf-brown suit
Of gathered underwear, and raised a foot
Above the ring of petticoats she regarded
Winsomely as they blossomed on the floor.
She looked like Peter Pan about to soar.

LXXVIII

Her dullish hair in clusters flocked along
Shoulders poised high as though held in suspense
For some delight to sunder her from sense
And stretch her voice out in orgasmic song.
She eyed me with abstraction, as to say:
'Oh, here's the one who's come to aid our play';

LXXIX

Then turned from me and did a pirouette,
Her hair flung out, her arms advanced, her eyes
Glassed with self-conscious rapture in surmise
Of satisfaction near. Denise — her sweet
Poking at me from lips which massaged it —
Slid up in bed beneath a clinging sheet

LXXX

Which immediately dropped. Her breasts sprang out
Like flowers in bloom blown into blowing light
And stood there hard, filling my fixed sight,
A moon for each eye in this night of doubt
Sucking and squeezing all my emptiness
In worlds of warmth defiant of distress.

LXXXI

Evangelina then embraced me first.
Theatrically one leg she hooked round
My waist. Her sprung hair brushed my face. She wound
Her arms about my neck, and I, immersed
In breathing flesh, felt th'other leg curl up
To join its partner in a scissor grip.

LXXXII

I was bowed and still as suns began to burst
Like dandelion-heads cut off by breath
From furnace-blasts not greying them in death
But cutting them live and neat from stalks a-thirst.
I heard myself give groan, and Denise listened,
As her big bombazine humbug twirled and glistened.

LXXXIII

Both girls enjoyed me. I enjoyed both girls.
Like a grinning trap open upon the moon
In a night of woe, my loins snapped oversoon
And released and released, — my eyes clouded with curls,
My ears moist with breath, my head with dreams
Springing red, gentian, white. I heard their screams.

LXXXIV

A red train like a dragon scraped the top
Of crags eaten in air by windy fire.
Flesh yanked on flesh in a dragging of desire.
The red train hurtled open and blew up.
Then sweet rain put the fires out; rest ensued,
And night's meadows spread into distance all moon-dewed.

215

LXXXV

I woke relieved — though grieving-grey the sky
Beyond the window. It was not a dream.
Four beds still faced each other in the gleam
Of morning. Neither girl was there, but I
Saw three beds had been slept and tussled in.
Each vacant sheet was ridged into a grin.

LXXXVI

I sheathed a moistened and delighted groin;
Dressed myself, whistling; and then felt as free
As I ever had been. Authority
Could not, with lack of my assent, enjoin
Me to some embarkation for a Dark
Tower far from strolls in a green park.

LXXXVII

No one constrained my actions. No one watched
Mt numb gyrations round the room.
I heard no threat'ning, hurried tramping come
To escort me between bayonets overarched.
I was free to run or settle as I would,
Or pirouette, or handstand, as I could.

LXXXVIII

I found my way quite easily to the hall
Of khaki where breakfast was being served.
I did not feel myself to be unnerved
By yesterday's proceedings after all
Yesterday's sober panic. I was free
As ever I had been, and free would be.

LXXXIX

I eat cold breakfast; swallowed sickening tea.
Faces about me were familiar —
Yet not the same as last night's faces here
In the twilit hall, though all appeared to be
Scooped from my recollection of a past
Wherein each face now present knew unrest.

216

XC

I hummed my way to the platform. Few folk stood
In isolated triangles as a breeze
Buffeted me and stroked into my eyes
Moment'ry tears whereby I felt good
— But for a moment only. The refugee
With a hat too large for him walked warily

XCI

In circles within a circle he had seen
Carved in the platform for him, though to all
Eyes but his own it was invisible.
There was no sign of others who had been
With me yesterday, nor had had I seen a
Sign of Denise and/or Evangelina.

XCII

The signals were all down against the sky
Like waiting birds; the which I took to be
Propitious of my regained liberty.
A porter with broom in hand came up to say:
"Are you for Portling?" — "Yes, I think I am."
"It'll be about five minutes. This platform."

XCIII

Why should I go to Portling? — Anywhere
Would do so long as I left Breakdown now.
Portling was a terminus, this I knew.
I would catch a train to any place from there
Resembling last week's cities blooming fine
With spearing spires and traffic'd streets divine.

XCIV

And soon the little train to Portling-Hoo
— Two words, "The Banner", looped and dashed in paint
Within the rondure of its squatting front —
Arrived and steamed and shook. About me blew
Gusts, captured into silence, then renewed.
I clanged a carriage-door against the cold.

217

XCV

The hostel slowly shed its visitors,
My fellow passengers of yesterday
Who did not seem inclined to move away
From Breakdown with its squares and corridors,
And all together gathered into groups; —
But soon boarded the train in lissom troops.

XCVI

I was alone in the carriage as it moved
From Breakdown Junction into land striken bare —
A plateau balding and torn by thinning air;
And rock, croft, girder, cottage, grasses, roved
Past at a decent speed. Soon the sea's line
Like a cable touched at intervals by sunshine

XCVII

Appeared between hillocks. Within the carriage
Wool protruded wirily from my seat,
And on the floor a wrapped, two-pointed sweet
Which had been spilt and left when someone's courage
Yesterday gave up, swayed in a grey
Stroke of sunlight that breathed and melted away.

XCVIII

After half an hour's travelling in descent
We levelled with the sea-line, and in due
Time, crawled lamely into Portling-Hoo.
I lowered a carriage window; as I leant
Out upon a dockyard scene, my blood
Froze for a second time, and then I stood,

XCIX

As once before, cold-chiselled out of wood.
At another platform facing me again
With windows like blind eyes was the red train,
Upon its sides the paint streaking like blood
Just spilt: announcing menaces and doom
Across two coaches' flanks, 'This is your Tomb!'

C

Slapdashed in garish letters, twisted, immense.
I fell out onto the platform; all about me,
Some looking worried, others nervously
Grinning, thronged, but all were in suspense.
Then red-cross personnel ushered this herd
(And me) into a Vaccination Ward.

CI

This was a massive room lit silver-bright
By many windows. Soon as I was there,
I saw one sitting, throned in a wheel-chair,
At the room's far end, and armoured all in light.
This was the God of War whose name is Mars,
And at his feet—her hair bound by stone stars—

CII

Was a beautiful grey-eyed lady whom I knew
To be Venus, Goddess of Love. The God had missing
Both arms, both legs; and lips unused to kissing
Except in rage and ravishing, bloomed blue
Above tight bandages. Before him stood
Upon a chessboard chessmen of rare wood.

CIII

He played the game with himself by calling out
The moves he wished to make, and also those
Made by unseen opponents. As he chose,
The august lady shifted the woods about
According to his will. She raised a hand—
"White: King to Bishop One," came the command.

CIV

She knew when he was just about to speak.
Her smile was not self-satisfaction
But rather gratitude for that within
Her supreme power always to further seek
Diversity in what she knew to be
Absolute—like Heavenly equity.

219

We stood in quietude about this pair.
Sometimes sunlight beat upon the dust
That sumptuously rolled its flecks of rust
And silver; sometimes, dark and still the air.
The bescarfed don came up to stand by me
And whispered: "The General and his Lady".

"Black: Pawn takes Pawn." Again the God had spoken.
The Goddess moved the pieces as he uttered.
About us a bright light with dust was shuttered
Which then swam free as briefly dust was broken.
The grey-eyed lady lifted a delicate hand—
"White: King takes Pawn," was the warrior's command.

Fewer and fewer folk now seemed within
The hall where dust and transitory sunlight
Swept meltingly together through a dun light
Grown peaceful, peaceful. The refugee was seen,
Broad-hatted, for a moment, in a fall
Of light that beamed then vanished from the hall.

"Black: Pawn to Bishop Six." Illnesses swarmed,
Bulbous-faced, in skirts of sinew, over
And within the gold- and silver-dusted hover,
Then vanished, dancing, leaving us unharmed.
The lady smiled and knew a perfect peace,
Stretching her limbs in dust with perfect ease.

And in the distance embarkation orders
Were being shouted somewhere. I was not
Willing, however, now to leave this spot.
In the room's corners four white-coated warders
Watched with dusty countenances the game
Dictated by Love's lover who was lame.

CX

"White: King to Rook Three. Black: the Bishop takes
"Knight Five." She kissed the pieces with her hand;
One more stood vanquished at the God's command.
She never knows satiety, but makes
Us think she does, I thought. We were alone,
The three of us, in dust white as scoured bone.

CXI

"White: King takes Bishop. Mate!" The God leaned back,
That formless cripple leaned back in his chair.
The lady smiled at him through the dim air.
He seemed as one relieved upon a rack.
And then the lady turned and smiled at me,
And peace and dust descended silently,

CXII

And dust was veined with light. The lady's gaze
Swept greyly over me and over him
Who stood beside me motionless in a swim
Of dust. No words were spoken. And now haze
Secluded all, as when light goes and eyes
Waken in sleep from dream to dark surprise.

CXIII

The world was empty of all but gulphs of sleep,
And all the gulphs were stitched with a voiceless road
On which no pilgrim leans towards his abode
Nor any conscious thought prevails the deep
Of an unending quiet. Only a sea
Whispers, with tides like breath, the word 'Mercy'.

The Remembered Angels

I remember the angel climbing
the roof of my house, its silver
bones gliding over the shingles
like rain, and I remember carving
my name on my bed where my parents
couldn't find it so when the angel
came to take me it would know
my name. I remember dying like that
night after night, preparing
for ascension to an empire
without smoke or wind or fire,
and I imagined my father walking
anxiously in front of the window
jingling the coins in his pockets,
raising on his feet as if his heels
were burning and my mother
with her sharp knife slicing apples,
arranging the slices like mirror images
of cheeks moist with juice too sweet
to be tears. I imagined the angel
saying drink this milk before bed,
it will ease your sleep. Leave the
stones where you found them they have
settled their places in the earth already.
No matter how dark the night or how bitter
my solitude, I saw the angel draped
in lace with white jewels in its hair
floating just above the mist
with a branch in its hand
pointing towards the stars. I knew
the angel was smiling and could see me
even under the many covers of my bed
and in my sleep I saw not one angel
but hundreds, all going in the other
direction, locking their hands together
like a wall of of sheet lightning that sliced
the dark air again and again, blocking
the road, and I saw myself the size
of a stone and motionless, seeing
the angels move down the road like that
all blind and singing.

The Roadmenders

"Through bankrupt countries where they
mend the roads." — W.H. Auden

Grandmothers mend the roads,
lifting their great pans high
heavy with sand or gravel.
They stoop in the dried-up river's
bed to dig the fill, squatting
to chop some stone as if
it were a garden cabbage.
Young girls mend the roads here,
sun drying them up like vines,
and their fruit goes withered
in fumes from lumbering buses
whose Punjabi drivers curse
to be caught in such lowlands
and hell, such potholes for wheels.
Such a ditch and these winding
trails should not exist,
dug out by hands because the flood
has broken the heart of a bridge,
refuted its excellent logic,
fractured its place in the landscape.
For the gods want the roads
worked on, the supernumerary,
crooked, leprous, accursed roads,
want penance for the lives
of these women, the lives
they spent elsewhere, dancing,
carousing with the mad emperor,
strolling in the green and cool gardens.
For such reasons, because of the gods
and their convictions against good bridges
and bad women, the formerly bad women
mend the roads, stooping in the sun,
lifting heavy mattocks and pans
upon their heads. And if they complete
one road they can begin another,
the one stretching off into the distance,
twisting like a lazy serpent in the sun.
And at night, let them braid
the long black hair of their daughters.

The Shaman

When the Shaman came to the village
It was after noon, and the people
Gathered slowly, leaving their fetid huts
With surly interest, shuffling
In groups towards the fenced enclosure
Where stripped trees shone
Like the debris of a dream.

He stood there and said nothing.
'This is the rainmaker from Kasang'
Announced the headman. 'He is here
To help us charge the sky
And understand the nature of our sin.
He will undertake a reckoning
And release the rains'.

The Shaman asked for food and solitude.
Taken to the prepared house
He rested for two hours.
Later, the people wanted to know
If he had prayed or interceded
In any way, not trusting
The absence of rhetoric.

Because the Shaman, leaving the house
Before sunset, had only stared
Towards the low line of hills
In the West, with his mouth open,
Breathing in the dead air of the village
With its sour urinal smell
Of a desolate people.

Then he walked away, his blanket
Neatly folded over one shoulder,
Almost marching, with his stick
Swinging jauntily above the ground.
'Why are you leaving us?' the people asked,
Aware that nothing had changed —
Not even themselves.

He paused impatiently but without drama
So that afterwards no-one remembered
The moment exactly — especially the words;
But they recalled the professional
Spareness of the man, his ordinary voice,
And the compactness
Of his authority.

'He told us' the headman explained later,
'That he was not necessary, as the rain
Would come soon of its own accord'.
Lacking all style and ambiguity,
The statement seemed both true and unacceptable,
An irrelevance that ignored
Their contract and their needs.

It left an impossible situation.
Certainly the fields were flooded
And the people did not starve.
They cleaned their houses and began
To forget the long drought and terrible emptiness
Of the time they had waited
For expiation and rain.

But they could not escape the difficult questions
That gnawed away their confidence
In a malevolent authority.
Perhaps the Shaman had deceived them
When he denied intervening
In their dry world
Of guilt and dust.

Or perhaps they had been punished enough
And had received a warning
About the sovereignty of death.
They toyed with ideas like these
But were undermined by the casual integrity
Of the Shaman when he walked away
Unrewarded into the night.

The Ships

bend their masts
to let in the view.

Harbors rise
from the earth

in winding sheets
of light. Men

pole flatboats
with their catch

through the long towers
of the city. Evening

turns on its side
like a white

swordfish
in a basket.

The Silence

Traces can be found towards the lough
and soon I hold
a full-grown silence in my sights:

a lack of sound more elderly and grand
than all the pines and birches
whose water-edge I share. It rests

across the lap of water like a blade,
separating trees and sky
from their reflecting selves. Perhaps

my bench of driftwood cracks: the silence
listens, turns and starts.
The geese are up and walk towards me,

shorewards on a plank of light: clumsily
they raise unruly wings,
breaking out their syllables like hounds.

The Site

(an extract)

Trucks bring the shingle that will form the bed
On which the pipes will rest. The dumpers shed
Their tinkling showers of stone. The banksman slings
On Ivan's chains the pipes and manhole rings.
With labours such as these the weeks roll by;
More trenches dug, pipes laid, the holes backfilled,
With junctions to insert, manholes to build,
Until, — the engineer consults his plan, —
It's time the building of the road began.
Then John the Pole, who lays the kerbs, is brought,
Respected by so many men he's taught,
The sturdy henchman of the kerbs he serves
In ramrod lines, in smoothly sweeping curves.
His confidence in every action shows
His skill; where novices may guess, he knows.
When John the Pole embarks on setting out
A road, a radius, a roundabout,
Half measured up, half judged by practised eye,—
Just as an alchemist of days gone by
Invoking spirits by his magic spells
Would draw his circles and his parallels,
His occult mysteries beheld with awe,
So all regard the lines that John will draw.
No wonder youngsters with their spurs to earn
Exclaim, Why, even John once had to learn!
The day comes when the bed of hoggin's made,
The gulley-pots put in, the conduits laid.

227

This is the day the gang have waited for
Impatiently: all's ready for the pour.
The mixer truck, a distant gleam of white,
Is hailed by Tom when first it comes in sight;
The lazy moment fled, alert they wait.
Still half at ease, the gang anticipate
The road their busy shovels will create,
That sudden burst of high activity,
The pressing need to do, and thus to be:
Just one more demonstration of the theme
That work establishes their self-esteem.
Truck after truck will come, discharge, and go.
The digger bucket sweeping to and fro
Will level mounds of concrete. Shovels fling
Lean mix around. There's endless shovelling.
At last the foreman with his line has checked
The camber or the crossfall is correct,
The concrete's rolled, the sealing compound sprayed:
Now dinner can no longer be delayed.
Relaxed, all troop into the wooden hut.
The conclave congregates, the door is shut.
Each has his box of sandwiches to eat
Ensconced at ease in his familiar seat
In some rough precedence of status owed
To time or skill, the gang's unspoken code.
Sometimes there's reminiscent talk of deeds
Sprung from the rowdy devilment that leads
Men into pranks and horseplay with their mates.
One caps the tale another man relates;
Events turn into legends of the sites.
The bumptious man's discomfiture delights,
But boasts or threats fulfilled will be acclaimed,—
Some adversary felled, or woman shamed.
Today they sit in silence, tired out,
The shovel thrown down at the foreman's shout
Of 'Dinner time!' The welcome half hour's break
Gives aching limbs time to recuperate:
Tea-mug in hand, sprawled out at length Tom lies,
While Bernie droops his head, with half-closed eyes
In drowsy rest. All in the hut is still,
All lost in hushed oblivion, until
The foreman rises, and at once his men
Are roused to brisk activity again.

High summer now; the dusty earth is dry
Beneath a parching desert-blue of sky.
Now sweating backs of supple bronze are bent
Beneath the weight of truckloads of cement.
More trenches open up, more pipes are laid,
And soon another stretch of road is made.
Who are these men, these nameless pioneers,
Whose handiwork may last a thousand years?
Let Peter speak, whose history portrays
How yesterday's decisions make today's:
'I'm just a common labourer', he said,
'I might have been a bricklayer instead.
I was apprenticed when I started first.
The work began to bore me. What was worst
Was having, say, a length of wall to build,
And when you'd done a job you thought was skilled
The foreman came and knocked it down again;
And all my pals were paid the rates of men.
With three years served, just eighteen months to go,
I left, — broke my apprenticeship, — and so
Became a labourer. That's seventeen
Years back. Since then I've done most things. I've been
A digger driver. Seven years of that
Was quite enough. It's not good when you're sat
In there all day, — the jolting and the noise!
I'm happier outside here with the boys'.
He took his shovel; out there in the sun
Another job was waiting to be done.

The Summer Of The Wild Artichokes

1.

That summer I found
a stain with two red lobes,
a heart's sediment in my underpants.
I carried them to my mother
and we kissed

229

in the heat of August
in Jerusalem, a kiss
like cool water
tainted with iron.

While the day's strikes over Suez
droned on the radio,
my mother smashed ice with a cleaver
and mashed apricots,
yellow as egg yolks, flecked with red;
the ice cream melting as I served the women
who pressed glasses of iced mint tea
to their brows, and called me "bat mitzvah."

That summer the wild artichokes
muscled their way
through scrub and brambles.
They stood four feet high,
bronze arms, gold dusted,
their crown of thistle
began to unlock
the gold fur patch
in the centre, spread,
not like sunflower's platters of seed,
but like suns.

We played paratroopers
in the Valley of the Cross, tumbled
out of olive trees casting
their immature green bullets down.
We scrambled through thistles,
fell into thornbushes,
hung by our knees, imagining
the long roll of sky
around us, and the earth below
winking in the pure light,
a gemmed map
before the scramble into crossfire.

2.

The school nurse comes for all the girls.
We follow her into the clinic.

She draws the shades,
looks outside the door, and locks it.
She tells us there is nothing to be ashamed of.
    "Your ovaries are about the size and shape
    of little plums,
    but your womb is like a pear upside-down."

The girls stuff braids into their mouths;
purple shadows quiver in their brown cheeks,
glee darts like fieldmice. Plums! Pears!
One whispers, "Compote,"
they clutch their dark, delicate knees
with white fingertips.
The nurse shrugs.
Soon, she thinks,
You'll be doing the explaining.
"Has any of you begun her bleeding?"

One raises her hand:
a tree has hushed them
in the shade of giant boughs.

During afternoon classes, helicopters
pass overhead, carrying
the wounded back from Sinai.
The sound whips
at the vortex of the sky
like an eggbeater.
As if in heavy fluid
our heads turn to the windows.
The history teacher draws the shades.

3.

Years later, in America,
I walk into a high school bathroom
which is silent and packed with girls
whose doughy faces are barred
with mascara, who suck
at cigarettes like convicts.
And there it is:
the drag of heavy fluid

toward a vortex where clattering panic
apes the heartbeat.
Someone said someone said a girl died
of lye poured in her womb
by an illegal abortionist.
Her memory seeps into the walls'
gradations of paint,
seeps into the painted faces
grading them with fear.

4.

A bomb blows in the supermarket.
Cases of tomato paste
blast into the street
with splintered sheetglass.
Among the swathes of red gum,
only one woman is hurt.
She lost her husband in '56,
her son in '67; now
she has lost her legs.
Everyone calls her *brave*.

We memorize the names
of things with bombs in them:
purses, buttons, candy, stuffed animals.
Names don't matter —
love, victory, State of Israel —
all wrap bombs. Between
the bomb and the wrapping,
the only thing left
unsuspect, is to act.

5.

In the gorge where we began
our hike: two red cliffs
split by a cataract
laddered with rainbows.
The booming water
filled a deep pool;

I stripped off my khaki
with the others, lying
open-eyed to the blue sky.
The water pounding down its shaft of foam
loaded my heart;
minnows nibbled the hairs
on my legs; when I moved
they drifted like fronds.
The net of being
kissed like sun on water;
then souls can breathe
through pores of rock
or minutes in the skin
of time, easily;
it is easy
to hallucinate words
in that kiss:
singing peels off waterfalls,
the heart's double chant
recalls what is to be.

6.

As we turn this corner
in the mercurial dust of evening
in Jerusalem, or elsewhere,
and you have somewhere to go
from the pitched noon
of your childhood,
and I also have new problems
in old countries,
still,
a word before we go
to light our lamps.

When they say
"Girls can't be paratroopers",
then you will know
it's too late, because
you walked out
and the street tilted under you;
studied the book

and fell through the lines;
in a word,
you jumped,

jerked the string, got tendons
for floating, and your parachute
englobes slowly like a winged cerebrum.
Whatever fell with you—
scraps of meat,
congealing tears—bat aside.
Now is the time to see
the whole pattern:
sand split with silver deltas,
forests and rivers branching
like neurons, the long scars of roads.
In that pure light
brushed by pinions
you angle toward the curve
crossburned and smoking, small
as a children's ditch,
small as human fury,
and you descend;

when the pure mind falls into battle
knowing what she knows,
the sun's thistles meet her, bronze and gold
with sisters' faces,
as her feet
join their shadows
for the long rush under fire.

Three-quarters

1.

I wasn't happy with aspects of my case.
I shut myself in the bathroom, a three-sided looking glass
open like a book. I couldn't understand my face.
My nose stuck out. I combed my hair down over my eyes
in search of a parting that would change my life.
I opened the mirror slowly, turning my head
from full to three-quarter face. I wanted to stand
three-quarters on to the world, in a slow, blind place —
out of reach. I sat in front of the sunray lamp
with pennies in my eyes. I dyed my skin
a streaky yellowish brown with permanganate of potash.
I must have grown up slowly in that looking-glass bathroom,
combing my hair straight down and pretending to wash.
I made myself dizzy raising my arms above my head
in a kind of surrender. No one else could get in.

2.

When I came downstairs my hair looked extraordinary —
a turmoil of popular styles and prejudices
stiff with unreality and fear.
My scalp stung from onsets of a steel flick-comb.
My parting was raw from realignment.
I'd reintroduced the casual look so many times
I'd forgotton what it was. The whole thing
looked like an instrument of self-torture
with a handle and a zip.

I made my entrance and everyone wanted to know
where I was off to looking like that.
My brother did a comb-mime with his knife,
tongue hanging out, jacket pushed back like a Ted.
My father made me go upstairs and start again.
I'd been working on my hair for so long
I thought it was natural to have a whirlpool
on your head, or a ship. I couldn't grasp the fact
that my hair was my hair, nothing more.

3.

As soon as they went out, I stood still
with the stuffed crocodile, wondering what to do.
Have a shot of creme de menthe from the bottle?
Or go upstairs and look for evidence of myself?
I'd seen it all before: the toilet case
of film-star cigarette cards, the bundles
of old theatre programmes, unfinished albums
from Eden Roc and Monkey Island Hotel.
I turned the pages slowly, listening for the car,
till my father was young again, a soldier,
or throwing back his head
on slicked-back Derby Days before the war.
I stared at all that fame and handsomeness
and thought they were the same.
Good looks were everything where I came from.
They made you laugh. They made you have a tan.
They made you speak with conviction.
'Such a nice young man!' my mother used to say.
'So good looking!' I didn't think they were,
but I searched my face for signs of excellence,
turning up my collar in the long mirror
and flourishing a dress sword at myself. I could see
I'd have to do more than that to satisfy my honour.

To The Cricket

Seducer, can your song
persist, keyed-up and long
as this unsleeping night?
The notion that it might,
that a spondaic chirr
is all that may occur
until the daylight rouses
birds in their penthouses—
the thought alone would keep
the mind astray from sleep.

Outdoors, but all too near
to an unwilling ear,
the friction of your knees
breeds importunities.
Please please meet me—your cry
wheedles each passer-by
to be your pampered guest
in a snug ivy nest.
For ever pitched the same,
you are immune to shame,
and never chirp the less
for nightlong unsuccess.

Is it the cleaner choice
not to give need a voice?
Your silent auditor
finds second thoughts a bore,
yet fields them even while
framing a chilly smile,
counting the hours gone
and yet to go till dawn,
glad to the point of fear
that none will ever hear
his wants—unweakening, vain—
confessed to counterpane.

Tremedda Farm

The worst storm of the year.

Rain polishing a cobbled yard
By night; while sharp winds stitch

Bright water into the eyelets
Of the stonework, driving the rain

Into the pocks and hollows
Where the crystal shows through.

In the howling weather
A fox pads the granite.

By dawn, it is still. The cobble
Spattered with a shiny green

Lard of chicken droppings
Reflecting the morning light; feathers

Festoon the yard, lumped into wet balls.
The fox, having savoured

The interior wetness of the fowl,
Lies somewhere, digesting the white meat

While the rain dries up,
His fur pearled with shining water.

Venus Moves House

Red brick, Victorian, two-up, two-down,
My first house stood opposite a banana factory;
Wedged between stout neighbours, it held its own.

I painted it and papered it, covered the cracks,
Hung Japanese lanterns against the dark,
And called it home. So did the cats.

There was the garden. Narrow vegetable beds
Run wild to leeks and pansies. Broken fences.
One old chimney pot. A tumbled shed.

I tore that down, despite a certain light
I liked that crept in at the window.
I left the pansies, yellow, purple, white,

Spilling at the edges. And cow parsley
Pushing through the fences. My garden,
Shaking a green head at the factory,

Rearranged her skirts. Transformation scene:
Hollyhocks, honeysuckle, Lad's Love, Thyme -
They grew contrariwise. And, where the shed had been,

A dancing Venus, leaning widdershins,
Scrambled with roses and with cockleshells
The Genius Loci on her home-made shrine.

She watched my garden grow. I brought her gifts:
Trees drifting blossoms like late falls of snow;
A purple butterfly bush; two ponds; and fish.

For a small space ours, this garden lent,
Like some rich garment borrowed, handed down,
Patched, darned and worn by each incumbent

Just a little differently. The garden's magic
Held me in its thrall, and held at bay
The ranting voices, the dull ache of traffic.

And then, a random venture. It was an idle curiosity
Drove me to see the cottage. I knew at once
That I would move, and leave behind me

The house, the garden: things made, things loved.
Moving and Removing: a continuous shift
Of small immemorabilia. Such stuff. Such stuff.

We take it with us; what we leave behind
Is something of ourselves, a way of dress
That soon will be forgotten. Never mind,

239

Parting is such sweet sorrow. So the rooms are stripped
To brick and mortar, wood and lath;
An emptiness that testifies to a strange gift

Given to those who travel far and light:
Knowledge that what is left behind, forgot,
Is precious, safe. Whatever comes by night.

And so I leave my garden. It will still be there
Whatever others add or take away.
Let them lay lawns, grow cabbages. Fair's fair,

Pansies do not give up so easily. Nor roses.
And somewhere in time and space my garden is,
Intact, for always. So, too, that first house

Across from the banana factory. I haunt its site
Switching furniture and curtains, casting other colours
Than its own, causing a certain light

To creep in at the window. Things left behind
Cling like burrs and cannot be removed.
The Past is. To move on is to find

The ghosts of others waiting at each corner,
Friendly, reticent, but there. Each needs his talisman,
So I brought Venus. After all, who can travel without her?

Villanelle: I Live With Losers

I live with losers, losers understand
and speak a language I need not translate:
home in my landscape they defend my land;

for losers light their loss and keep it fanned:
a black house can't afford an empty grate:
I live with losers, losers understand.

240

Yet losers laugh when laughter comes to hand:
loss is not poker-faced in solemn state.
Home in my landscape they defend my land

where losers cry and crying is not banned,
for we are groundless and we have no weight.
I live with losers, losers understand.

No loser claims existence can be bland:
(snow bites, abrasive, and fire tears like hate)
home in my landscape they defend my land.

Loss grows no skin to graft over the brand
and holds no passport to a sweeter state.
I live with losers, losers understand:
home in my landscape they defend my land.

Walking To Mountains
With Gary Snyder

We cross the county after work to hear Gary Snyder.
It's the day after they've forced night in, and
The October fog lifts in all the wrong places.
Though truckers tend to drive at night on North Devon roads
So as not to get caught up with other traffic,
It's all right, and we have time for a beer.

In the hotel, a couple play pool, local barflies
Buzz. Otherwise the place is empty. We
Brave it out, like the travellers we are: you
Crack jokes for the first time in months.
The effort has worked a magic on us:
Our trip has become a quest.

I'd never believed the photographs. To me he was
Long and lean always. He
Wore a check shirt maybe, and blue jeans, and carried

Just enough in a well packed rucksack . . .
To me he was the shape to keyhole freedom.
To me, he was me.

In those days, Asiamerica was the territory
Our thoughts belonged to. O.K., there were the Beatles, but
Christ, I was always walking to mountains with Snyder,
We all were: with our Dhammapadas and our
Joss sticks and our copies of Milton
By firelight we walked a thousand miles.

We yelled his ideals while others sustained
Tax systems, hard-sell advertising,
M-Way projects, while New Towns goliathed:
Sleeping in derelict houses in Southern conurbations,
Camped out penniless by Northern forests, we
Discussed the life he recommended and lived, endlessly.

And we're all here tonight, aren't we?
Out they've come, the kaftans, the milkmaid brocades,
The never-relinquished duffles, the beards -
Encouraged for occasions of exactly this kind -
The long earth-mother dresses, the army surplus
Greatcoats, the special ways of keeping hair.

We are back now when walking any street it seemed
A smile could win smiles, when you could
Greet complete strangers so freely
That it sometimes got embarrassing. We are back
In the communes of the New Age,
With Timothy Leary, among 'heads', acid, and cosy anarchy.

None here think it strange, how people come and sediment to
A compromise with fashion, with style;
How, deciding 'This is the way I shall live,
Forever', one will forever buy that sort of shoe,
That make of special blue denim,
Roll precisely that kind of cigarette.

He unwraps his books. So many did,
I remember, unwrap things from silk
Kerchiefs as though, like Whittington,
They had nothing more. He unwraps his books

Carefully, placing them
Around, as though we should understand,

And introduces himself quietly,
In a voice that only just carries
To the rear of the hall. At once I am back:
I am back by campfires and wondering,
Wondering . . . maybe . . . Maybe it was all
Easy for him in the mountains,

And maybe he didn't know about us in Luton,
About our money troubles, and the sort of life we had?
It becomes important to me to know that
He knew what it was like in the poorer parts of English towns,
That he himself had broken loose from them,
That I had broken loose . . . I get confused

Because I am my own person now, and no longer
Walk to mountains with light sack and
Eastern texts; because I live in Devon, England;
Because I have just taken on a mortgage;
Because I learned not to love so freely.
Because I left a past behind me . . .

He reads his poem about the full moon
In the centre of the sky, about
The Equinox, the Equator. About how
Some things can only happen in one place,
At one time. And isn't there something of
Destiny about an evening

In which I start, desperately, to long for the time,
The gushing time, when, they said, we 'got it all
Wrong, for the right reasons':
When we were unafraid to have heroes,
When to shout their names seemed sufficient
Reason for being in a place?

Returning, I don't see any fog whatever.
I talk to you, we converse. I say 'There's probably
A full moon!' but neither of us is sure.
At midnight we kick into the Kentucky:
I feel whole, joined up: we buy enough for
One, two, three thousand miles.

243

WE, the Second ANZACs

Frontstalag 183
Salonika, 1941

Empty shell of cavalry barracks on hill
looks down on town, flanked
by black needles of cypress guarding white crosses.

Eyeless heat beats down, squirming vermin
pressing back; noble pile outside, festering within,
only held together by bugs in the plaster linking hands.

To this shelter the prisoners come.

Anonymous thousands pass inside tinsel - sparkling wire -
to find cut-off emptiness, sunbleached
parade-ground unspeakably Greek.
From the railway station below, the Nazis
having stripped shops granaries and fields
of all food, ship Rice Corn Currants
Wine Grapes Olive Oil Tomatoes Copper
Rubber and Brass Fittings by train loads -
back to Deutschland;

this year's harvest, next year's sustenance
for the Greeks. People back home
can have no idea of the future horror
this ultimate will bring in sun-drenched
misery under this "New Order" in Europe.

We survive only in rigid discipline,
queing in companies of a hundred
waiting for a miracle . . . of Loaves and Fishes,
as our hunger-keened nostrils sniff
windborne aroma - fried fish for breffkuss
in the German cookhouse a mile away.

Strictly in daily rota we take hopeful turns
in tens for the Back-Up
of Gash Loop-the-Loop . . .
a possible second helping of the Soup left over.

The stirrer stirs steady from the Bottom,
else there's shouts. The Ladle is so heavy
with watchful eyes, it spills nervously.
"Look, that lucky sod's got a piece of meat!"

We know what we are fighting for;
but by their actions these ordinary Jerries
reject their Fuehrer, in compassion and by stealth.
And we are strengthened in our resolve.

Two Germans were killed on the road
near here last week; a lorry driver
and his mate, second line troops.

From Lahanas, the nearest village
they took thirteen hostages
and hanged them by thin cord
a few inches from the ground.

And laughing Yiannitza?
They do not hang out patriotic flags now
or sing the Woodpecker song, that hung
Mussolini up by the short hairs.

Or the lonely shepherd in his kaross
standing like some great bear in the mist
amidst the asphodel in the ruins of Pella,
ready to put to the knife the tenderest
of his flock, "For the sake of an Englishman"
just as his forebears had done for Great Alexander,
refusing payment. To skin it before your eyes
classically inflating beneath the fleece
by mouth in the age-old method.
How would these gorillas treat him?

Private Thomas Williams of The Welch,
'Taffy' to us, turns to cast-down Dai Evans,
dreaming of Maerdy, "We could do with a brew,
Dai boy. Shall I put the dixy on?"

Dai's scowl cracks to a smile;
the grey cottages that twist round the cwm
un-ravel from his brow.
There is no tea . . . of course.

245

Even in broad daylight, one dreams . . . with eyes open.

"Come, Celia. Today is your birthday.
Let us walk over the Heath to The Spaniard's.

Kicking the russet leaves beneath our flying feet,
hand in hand, we breast steep rise of Ken Wood
to stand silent in silent in half embrace overlooking the ponds,
recalling fragrant heather of Sugar Loaf, with you marooned
in Moscow, if there had been war. And I half-crazy
with fear for you, pacing up South Hill Park
stopping my ears to every wireless - "I have brought back
this Piece of Paper. Peace for Our Time!"

No peace and not for Our Time!

To look at me now, Celia you would not recognise
this sorry, dysentrical skeleton in these K.D. rags
Small wonder, you went back to Dublin
to marry Prendergast. Cerements do not become a bride."

And I am left all hollow, for emptiness of you,

as pain becomes a blur, to clutch that sudden twinge
at heart mere thought can induce.

But woman is flesh and flesh is grass
to shiver and respond to any carressing breeze.

There is no future in us.

One blue quinine tablet a day from Greek Red Cross,
a less occasional slice of fresh bread
or a tomato prove we are not forgotten.
One dreams of the sunlit peace of a green English village
with bicycles leant outside the general store.
One has endless time to do it.

SALONIKA — AUGUST, 1941

"On 12th April, the 6th Australian Division
and the New Zealand Division, hitherto called the
1st Australian Corps, became known as the Anzac Corps."

WAVELL, Despatch, 5th September 1941.

This W.W.II. revival of the historic name was only effected on the map at G.H.Q. It never made the shoulder tabs! For in those few short days in the April of 1941, the Anzac Corps. were already in action in the mountain passes of Northern Greece, struggling desperately to keep back the huge weight of armour, with which the Nazis had already struck down unprepared Yugoslavia. Overshadowed by larger events, the first Greek Campaign of '41 has now been almost forgotten; although, compared with the heroic muddle of the defence of Crete, it was a classic campaign of its kind. For those of the "Second" Anzacs, who took part in both, it will never be forgotten.

Neither will Salonika - Front Stalag 183; for it was through its barbed wire gates there, in the long, hot summer of '41, that passed nearly 20,000 Anzac and British prisoners-of-war, taken in Greece and Crete, on their way to the hardship and internment in Nazi Germany, that was to last for almost nearly four years. It was during that time together, an Anzac spirit really grew up and flourished.

The logistical problems of the Eastern Campaign imposed considerable demands on the rolling stock of the Nazi railway system, and the transportation of these new prisoners to Germany was brought to a stand-still for some months. It was in this period that Salonika became the apprentice ground for the prisoners to appreciate the nature of the ordeal before them.

It was to last four years.

This poem represents in part the experiences and thoughts of one of them.

Word Concerto In Three Flats

First Movement

Tempo comodo

Goodness knows there will ♭e ♭abies ♭orn
In droves
   In the years to come
   And a handful of them will become musicians
   In one way or another
   While an armful will be charmed
   By the Muse of Muses
   But how many thousands will saunter through the world
   Completely oblivious to
‖: The art that starts with a sparrow's cheep
And pinnacles with little children's laughter :‖

A Piacere

   To be sure the transcription
   Of hand-made music
   Has not been ignored by the world
   Or so it would seem from a casual walk
   Down any road or country lane

Graziozo

   For, to begin where begin the builders of houses,
   The very bricks of civilisation are laid
   Row upon row
   Side by side
   In a familiar pattern
   That can be taken for nothing else but a page
   Of written music, Granted,
   There are no lines or crotchets or quavers
   On brick walls
   But perhaps these are the sort of staves
   That leave something to the imagination
   The kind of music that measures the pauses
   Rather than treasures the tones
   Beat for beat.

The ancient abacus has all the notes and lines
Neatly strung beads
That legend relates were the roots of arithmetic
Perhaps it is not coincidence
That in musical notation
The key of four flats
A flat
Has its flattened notes
B
E
A
D

Second Movement

G. Major
Andante Scherzoso

Anything strung
On wires or strings
May be music, of course

Three strand pearls
Native beads
Pegs on clothes-lines
But the ultimate in animated notation
Must surely be the common-or-garden
Tram
Which bears its crotchets aloft
On one long note
Only changing the pitch when it turns a corner
Or rounds a bend

Third Movement

Cadenza

¹²₄ Do we really live in a world
Where everything is laid out
As precisely as a sheet of music
With only occasional improvisation?
Do we really live in a place
Where even the match-sticks are
Passable crotchets
The candles are
Fair minims
And toffee-apples
Lollipops
Boiled sweets and
Wrapped sweets
Are respectively
Minims
Crotchets and
Semibreves and
Breves

Pastorale in C Minor

Giocoso

§ All these symbols must have originated in nature
somehow
Perhaps the Great Semibreve is really the *Sun*
Maybe the lesser notes with their stems are raindrops
Or roses
Roses, I think, then the five-line stave could be
The rain pouring on the flowers:

250

Nice it would be to have sunshine with us
For all time!
(It occurs to me that the sun
Crossing the heavens
Defines a musical pause)

𝄐
Coda
Espressivo
A Tempo

𝄆 Perhaps we do
Perhaps the song of the living "universe"
Sings always
Whether or not there is someone else
There to hear it
Or something
Upon which
The song is written
Fine! 𝄇

You

You have an address: north.
One corner of North
and East.

I have next to my mouth
the steep of your chest, the damp hair
circling your wrist.

You remind me of a narrow plain
hidden by trees.

251

I met you in a store.
You asked, "Will you hold
my hips while I jump
down from these shelves?"

Walking backward
into mud, we discovered
the tread
of our shoes, its surprising
delicacy—one of the shoes
you were later to rescue
from a moving stream.

Suddenly you are a compass needle,
trembling.

A part of the world where silence
has nothing in it
but you: houses and towns.
A man.

Your first finger tracing
my eyes.

A map where hemispheres lie down
at once becomes a globe, spinning.

A space
where I find you
gone.

Body of water, body of land.
Night where it is cold.

Names of the Authors, and Prize-Winners

About the Arvon Foundation

Arvon was formed in 1969 to provide opportunity for young or aspiring writers and poets to meet and work with established writers—and to do this not in an institutional context but in a live situation near as possible to that most natural of all, the home and workroom of the established writer.

In the years that followed, as the demand for Arvon gradually grew, it became apparent that this enterprise in pursuing its original aim was making two other specific contributions.

The first was to the tutors, the established writers and poets (Arvon has now employed more than 400, the majority of whom have become constant supporters). The fees are not spectacular but many writers still find the work at Arvon a way of earning some money, a way that is compatible with their own work. Equally, the majority value the opportunity 'to get out of themselves' and contact an interested public; and it would seem that virtually all find that the opportunity to teach in this way satisfies a constituent part of their vocation.

The second is the least measurable but arguably the most substantial of Arvon's contributions. Some eight to nine hundred people visit the two centres each year. Only very few of these are seeking to become professional writers. Most often they are people deeply interested in and open to imaginative literature. Almost without exception their time at Arvon is a revelation to them. Their being introduced to disciplines and standards of work, being encouraged to exercise these, discovers for them a fresh appetite for literature. Out of having written exactingly they discover a new confidence in their judgement, and the possibility of far more rewarding response and delight. Eight or nine hundred members of the population could be dismissed as a drop in the ocean, but when one considers that the geniune poetry-reading public in this country can be measured in hundreds then this contribution over the last thirteen years may well have been priceless.

Is it though extravagant to claim that among the writing courses and training schemes Arvon and its experience is so uniquely formative? Time and again the letters of tutors and students support this claim. And it does seem increasingly substantiated by the number of Arvon students who support readings and poetry competitions, and also by the spontaneous formation of the now 300 strong Friends of Arvon.

The strength of Arvon is two-fold. One is the absolute simplicity of its formula. Each course breaks new ground not because it employs a new idea but because it unfolds out of the interplay of the unique authority of the individual tutors with the response of an unprecedented group of students. Arvon does no more than afford this unique interplay appropriate time and space. The other resource is quite simply, and still astonishing after all these years, the absolute commitment of the tutors—commitment not to Arvon *per se* but, unavoidable it would appear, to the questioning and excitement of the students.

The policy of Arvon, then, is inescapable: to preserve this simple formula; to make the courses known and available to as many interested people as possible (and this involves constant search for funds to enable people to attend who haven't the necessary means); and to provide as many sympathetic writers as possible, regardless of their 'literary denomination' or bent, with this opportunity to teach.

It is frequently suggested to Arvon that its activity is properly the concern of the Education Authorities. No one who has been involved in Arvon has any respect for this view. What happens at Arvon is integral to the art and practice of writing; and the proof that there is no place for this inside the education system is that when Arvon's activity is simulated in an educational context (whether school, institution or residential centre) the quality is diluted and the results are incomparably less valuable. If this were not the case there would never have been a demand for Arvon, nor any conceivable motive for bringing it into being. At the same time Arvon has always seen itself as non-exclusive and as complementary to educational concerns, and has sought to present its centres as pieces of specialist equipment that the Educational Authorities are encouraged to make use of.

Finally, it is sometimes suggested that Arvon's concern with the craft of writing is actually unhelpful to literature—that there are enough writers already, and that what writers and writing need is more readers. This suggestion is cynical and ill-conceived. True literacy can exist only where there is real command in the use of language. Literature, virtually by definition, is not conceivable to a less than literate society. In this country the level of literacy among the educated (which is of course a higher proportion of the community than ever before) is probably lower than it has been for a thousand years. Arvon by livening people to the rewards and the rigours of the craft of self-expressive creative writing is helping to restore geniune literacy—and that can only result in a greater and more informed appetite for literature.

John Moat, Co-Founder of the Arvon Foundation.

The Arvon Foundation has two centres: Totleigh Barton in Devon and Lumb Bank in West Yorkshire. Further details about Arvon and its courses can be obtained from:

Arvon Foundation

Totleigh Barton
Sheepwash, Beaworthy
Devon EX21 5NS
Tel: 040923 338

Lumb Bank
Heptonstall, Hebden Bridge
West Yorkshire HX7 6DF
Tel: 0422 843714